TARGET YOUR MATHS

Year 3

Stephen Pearce

Elmwood Education

First published 2014 by
Elmwood Education
Unit 5 Mallow Park
Watchmead
Welwyn Garden City
Herts. AL7 1GX.
Tel. 01707 333232

ISBN 9781 906 622 275

Numerical answers are published in a separate book.

Typeset and illustrated by Tech-Set Ltd., Gateshead, Tyne and Wear.

PREFACE

Target your Maths has been written for pupils in Year 3 and their teachers.

The intention of the book is to provide teachers with material to teach the statutory requirements set out in the Year 3 Programme of Study for Mathematics in the renewed 2014 National Curriculum Framework

In the renewed Framework the Year 3 Programme of Study has been organised into seven domains or sub-domains.

> Number – number and place value
> Number – addition and subtraction
> Number – multiplication and division
> Number – fractions
> Measurement
> Geometry – properties of shape
> Statistics

The structure of **Target your Maths 3** corresponds to that of the Year 3 Programme of Study. There is also a Review section at the end of the book.

All the statutory requirements of the Year 3 Programme of Study are covered in **Target your Maths 3**. Appendix I of the Teacher's Answer Book matches the statutory requirements and some essential non-statutory guidance with the relevant pages in this book. Most requirements are covered by more than one page. The author believes it is important that teachers have ample material from which to select.

Each single or double page lesson in this book is divided into four sections:

Introduction: the learning intention expressed as a target and, where necessary, clearly worked examples.

Section A: activities based upon work previously covered. This generally matches the requirements for Year 2 pupils. This section can be used to remind children of work previously covered, as well as providing material for the less confident child.

Section B: activities based upon the requirements for Year 3 pupils. Most children should be able to work successfully at this level.

Section C: activities providing extension material for the faster workers and for those who need to be moved quickly onto more challenging tasks. The work in this section generally matches the requirements for Year 4 pupils. Problems in Section C can also provide useful material for discussion in the plenary session.

The correspondence of the three sections A–C to the requirements for different year groups provides a simple, manageable structure for planning differentiated activities and for both the formal and informal assessment of children's progress. The commonality of the content pitched at different levels also allows for progression within the lesson. Children acquiring confidence at one level find they can successfully complete activities at the next level.

There is, of course, no set path through either the Year 3 Programme of Study or **Target your Maths 3** but teachers may find Appendices II and III in the Teacher's Answer Book useful for planning purposes. In these tables one possible approach is given to the planning of the curriculum throughout the year.

In Appendix II the **Target your Maths** pages for each domain are organised into a three term school year. In Appendix III the work for each term is arranged into twelve blocks, each approximately corresponding to one week's work. For the sake of simplicity blocks are generally based upon one domain only.

The structure as set out in Appendices II and III enables teachers to develop concepts progressively throughout the year and provides pupils with frequent opportunities to consolidate previous learning.

The author is indebted to many colleagues who have assisted him in this work. He is particularly grateful to Sharon Granville and Davina Tunkel for their invaluable advice and assistance.

Stephen Pearce

CONTENTS

TARGET   To read and write numbers to 1000 in numerals and in words.

1 one	9 nine	17 seventeen	60 sixty
2 two	10 ten	18 eighteen	70 seventy
3 three	11 eleven	19 nineteen	80 eighty
4 four	12 twelve	20 twenty	90 ninety
5 five	13 thirteen	21 twenty-one	100 hundred
6 six	14 fourteen	30 thirty	1000 thousand
7 seven	15 fifteen	40 forty	
8 eight	16 sixteen	50 fifty	

The way we read a digit depends upon its position in the number.

Examples

39 reads *thirty-nine*

392 reads *three hundred and ninety-two*

3926 reads *three thousand nine hundred and twenty-six*

A

	24		43		61				97
15	28			56	69			80	
		32	47				74	85	

1 Look at the Bingo card. Write each of the numbers in words.

These numbers are called out in the next game. Write each number in figures.

2 thirty

3 fifty-nine

4 twenty-one

5 seventy-six

6 seventeen

7 forty-two

8 ninety-eight

9 thirteen

10 fifty-four

11 eighty-seven

12 sixty-five

13 ninety-one

14 seventy-three

15 thirty-eight

16 forty-six

17 Write the amount of each cash prize in words.

£50   £100   £200   £500   £1000

3

B
Copy the table, writing each distance in figures.

	City	Road Distance to London (miles)
1	Amsterdam	three hundred and six
2	Barcelona	nine hundred and thirty-nine
3	Berlin	six hundred and fifty-seven
4	Brussels	two hundred and three
5	Copenhagen	seven hundred and forty-one
6	Nice	eight hundred and thirty-five
7	Paris	two hundred and fifty-seven
8	Venice	nine hundred and twelve
9	Vienna	seven hundred and sixty-four
10	Zurich	five hundred and ninety-seven

Venice

The figures below show the distance between London and other places in Great Britain.
Write each distance in words.

11 Aberdeen 887 km   14 Carlisle 506 km   17 Liverpool 348 km
12 Birmingham 195 km   15 Glasgow 661 km   18 Newcastle 459 km
13 Cardiff 247 km   16 Inverness 930 km   19 Nottingham 208 km

C
1 Copy and complete the table.

City	Distance to London (miles)	
Cairo	two thousand one hundred and eighty-three	
Tokyo	five thousand nine hundred and fifty-six	
Abu Dhabi	three thousand four hundred and four	
Singapore	six thousand seven hundred and forty-eight	
Beijing	five thousand and seventy-two	
Moscow		1557
Jerusalem		2246
New York		3469
Buenos Aires		6901
Delhi		4178

2 Use these digits. Make as many four-digit numbers as you can with a value of less than 5000.
Write the numbers:
a) in figures   b) in words.

2 9 0 4

TARGET To recognise the place value of each digit in a 3-digit number.

Example

548   The 5 has a value of 500.   Knowing the value of the digits means that you
       The 4 has a value of 40.   are able to partition numbers.
       The 8 has a value of 8.   548 = 500 + 40 + 8

A

Copy and complete by filling in the boxes.

1. 52 = 50 + ☐
2. 81 = 80 + ☐
3. 37 = ☐ + 7
4. 19 = ☐ + 9

5. ☐ = 60 + 4
6. ☐ = 90 + 6
7. 28 = 20 + ☐
8. 73 = 70 + ☐

9. 45 = ☐ + 5
10. 57 = ☐ + 7
11. ☐ = 10 + 3
12. ☐ = 80 + 9

13. 35 = 30 + ☐
14. 91 = 90 + ☐
15. 42 = ☐ + 2
16. 26 = ☐ + 6

17. ☐ = 70 + 8
18. ☐ = 50 + 4
19. 39 = 30 + ☐
20. 67 = 60 + ☐

B

What is the value of the underlined digit?

1. 2<u>7</u>5
2. 52<u>7</u>
3. 1<u>9</u>6
4. <u>3</u>41
5. 41<u>2</u>
6. 1<u>6</u>7
7. 53<u>8</u>
8. <u>2</u>84
9. 7<u>5</u>6
10. 80<u>5</u>
11. 3<u>2</u>3
12. <u>6</u>92

Partition these numbers as in the example.

13. 143
14. 471
15. 358
16. 216
17. 982
18. 709
19. 465
20. 534
21. 398
22. 526
23. 273
24. 945
25. 419
26. 653
27. 804
28. 781

Copy and complete.

29. 532 = 500 + ☐ + 2
30. 268 = ☐ + 60 + 8
31. 329 = 300 + ☐ + 9
32. 897 = 800 + 90 + ☐

C

What is the value of the underlined digit?

1. 24<u>6</u>1
2. 6<u>2</u>93
3. 178<u>5</u>
4. <u>3</u>137
5. 90<u>5</u>6
6. <u>4</u>570
7. 5<u>8</u>29
8. 230<u>4</u>
9. <u>7</u>618
10. 19<u>8</u>2
11. 324<u>7</u>
12. 6<u>5</u>34

Work out:

13. 1364 + 400
14. 3895 + 50
15. 2528 + 3000
16. 1746 + 500

17. 3273 + 40
18. 4031 + 5000
19. 6489 + 60
20. 2906 + 200

21. 3157 + 4000
22. 1642 + 600
23. 5394 + 2000
24. 2561 + 70

TARGET   To recognise the place value of each digit in a 3-digit number.

Example

716   The 7 has a value of 700.   Give the value of the underlined digit.

The 1 has a value of 10.   5<u>9</u>3 → 90   83<u>7</u> → 7

The 6 has a value of 6.   <u>2</u>78 → 200   4<u>5</u>2 → 50

A

Copy and complete by filling in the boxes.

1 45 = 40 + ☐

2 62 = 60 + ☐

3 28 = ☐ + 8

4 53 = ☐ + 3

5 ☐ = 10 + 7

6 ☐ = 80 + 9

7 71 = 70 + ☐

8 94 = 90 + ☐

9 56 = ☐ + 6

10 48 = ☐ + 8

11 ☐ = 70 + 5

12 ☐ = 30 + 1

13 24 = 20 + ☐

14 93 = 90 + ☐

15 67 = ☐ + 7

16 52 = ☐ + 2

17 ☐ = 30 + 9

18 ☐ = 40 + 6

19 22 = 20 + ☐

20 74 = 70 + ☐

B

What is the value of the underlined digit?

1 6<u>8</u>3   7 <u>9</u>06

2 <u>1</u>57   8 47<u>2</u>

3 51<u>9</u>   9 <u>2</u>34

4 9<u>4</u>1   10 10<u>7</u>

5 <u>3</u>25   11 8<u>6</u>1

6 79<u>8</u>   12 <u>7</u>43

Copy and complete.

13 376 = 300 + ☐ + 6

14 959 = ☐ + 50 + 9

15 ☐ = 200 + 90 + 5

16 ☐ = 400 + 8

17 523 = ☐ + 20 + 3

18 697 = ☐ + ☐ + 7

19 ☐ = 700 + 2

20 ☐ = 800 + 50

Partition these numbers.

21 384   25 751

22 968   26 873

23 415   27 696

24 129   28 244

C

Write down the value of the underlined digit.

1 3<u>4</u>21   7 3<u>5</u>07

2 <u>2</u>049   8 70<u>3</u>6

3 970<u>5</u>   9 2<u>6</u>54

4 55<u>8</u>9   10 <u>4</u>201

5 8918   11 106<u>9</u>

6 <u>6</u>163   12 63<u>9</u>2

Work out:

13 7820 + 50

14 5403 + 3000

15 8179 + 500

16 9264 + 40

17 3788 + 2000

18 1932 − 30

19 3616 − 400

20 4891 − 2000

21 5177 − 60

22 2533 − 500

23 7985 + 350

24 9659 − 2400

25 3274 + 1004

26 1728 − 701

27 9862 + 140

TARGET To use an understanding of place value to partition numbers in different ways.

Examples

637

$$637 = 600 + 30 + 7$$
$$= 500 + 130 + 7$$
$$= 400 + 230 + 7$$
and so on

$$637 = 600 + 37$$
$$637 = 630 + 7$$
$$637 = 607 + 30$$

A

Copy and complete.

1. $45 = 40 + \square$
2. $79 = 70 + \square$
3. $24 = \square + 4$
4. $52 = \square + 2$

5. $91 = 90 + \square$
6. $18 = 10 + \square$
7. $83 = \square + 3$
8. $36 = \square + 6$

9. $65 = \square + \square$
10. $27 = \square + \square$
11. $54 = \square + \square$
12. $49 = \square + \square$

Continue the patterns for three more lines.

13. $75 = 70 + 5$
$= 60 + 15$
$= 50 + 25$

14. $84 = 80 + 4$
$= 70 + 14$
$= 60 + 24$

15. $98 = 90 + 8$
$= 80 + 18$
$= 70 + 28$

B

Partition these numbers.

1. 746
2. 329
3. 972
4. 143
5. 615
6. 268
7. 893
8. 587

Continue the patterns.

9. $925 = 900 + 20 + 5$
$= 800 + 120 + 5$
$= 700 + 220 + 5$

10. $863 = 800 + 60 + 3$
$= 700 + 160 + 3$
$= 600 + 260 + 3$

Copy and complete.

11. $385 = 380 + \square$
12. $576 = \square + 76$
13. $723 = 700 + \square$
14. $647 = \square + 7$
15. $462 = 402 + \square$
16. $959 = \square + 9$
17. $238 = 230 + \square$
18. $814 = \square + 14$
19. $395 = 300 + \square$
20. $681 = \square + 80$

C

Partition these numbers.

1. 1742
2. 4316
3. 2893
4. 7679
5. 3531
6. 6285
7. 9427
8. 5968

Copy and complete.

9. $4845 = 4840 + \square$
10. $7583 = \square + 83$
11. $2921 = 2900 + \square + 1$
12. $8269 = 8000 + \square$

13. $5356 = \square + 356$
14. $3782 = 3000 + \square + 82$
15. $9647 = 9600 + \square$
16. $1974 = \square + 4$
17. $6739 = 6000 + \square + 9$
18. $2163 = 2000 + \square$
19. $4252 = 4200 + \square + 2$
20. $7571 = \square + 71$
21. $3486 = 3000 + \square + 6$
22. $1214 = 1200 + \square$
23. $5697 = \square + 7$
24. $9329 = 9000 + \square + 29$

TARGET To compare and order numbers up to 1000.

Examples

Put these numbers in order, smallest first.   384   438   348
Look at the hundreds first.   384   438   348
If the hundreds are the same look at the tens.   384   348
The correct order is 348, 384, 438.

A

Which number is smaller?

1 38 or 83
2 92 or 29
3 74 or 47
4 54 or 45
5 23 or 32
6 87 or 78

Which number is larger?

7 53 or 35
8 79 or 97
9 85 or 58
10 43 or 34
11 89 or 98
12 65 or 56

Copy and complete by filling in any numbers in the boxes so that the numbers are in order.

13 55 ☐ ☐ 60 61
14 ☐ 38 ☐ 41 45
15 79 ☐ 85 90 ☐
16 48 ☐ ☐ 51 52
17 100 97 ☐ ☐ 89
18 72 ☐ 70 ☐ 68

B

Which number is smaller?

1 256 or 265
2 734 or 74
3 468 or 486
4 312 or 321
5 85 or 835
6 689 or 698

Which number is larger?

7 346 or 364
8 595 or 559
9 28 or 278
10 432 or 423
11 976 or 967
12 845 or 854

Put these numbers in order, starting with the smallest.

13 912 845 921 854
14 375 357 294 249
15 543 682 534 628
16 763 817 871 736

What multiples of 10 lie between:

17 236 and 263
18 683 and 715?

C

Which number is larger?

1 3492 or 2943
2 2657 or 2567
3 963 or 6938
4 5269 or 5296
5 7541 or 7451
6 8786 or 8687

Put these numbers in order, smallest first.

7 954 3549 3459 945
8 2368 836 2386 863
9 7148 784 7184 748
10 2965 2956 2569 2659

What number is halfway between:

11 5600 and 5700
12 2420 and 2500
13 3400 and 4000
14 1960 and 2000

Use these digits once each.

5 8 6 2

15 Make the largest number possible.
16 Make the smallest number possible.

TARGET To find 10 or 100 more or less than a given number.

Examples

52 + 10 = 62   478 + 10 = 488   478 + 30

52 + 100 = 152   478 + 100 = 578

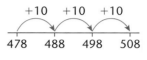

52 − 10 = 42   478 − 10 = 468   478 − 200

                      478 − 100 = 378

A

Work out

1. 23 + 10
2. 59 + 10
3. 77 + 10
4. 41 + 10

5. 36 − 10
6. 72 − 10
7. 98 − 10
8. 63 − 10

9. 35 + 10
10. 80 + 10
11. 12 + 10
12. 66 + 10

13. 47 − 10
14. 50 − 10
15. 84 − 10
16. 29 − 10

17. 74 + 20
18. 38 + 20
19. 95 − 20
20. 61 − 20

B

Work out

1. 285 + 10
2. 407 + 10
3. 354 + 10
4. 733 + 10

5. 248 + 100
6. 529 + 100
7. 861 + 100
8. 690 + 100

9. 125 − 10
10. 579 − 10
11. 942 − 10
12. 686 − 10

13. 609 − 100
14. 368 − 100
15. 752 − 100
16. 431 − 100

17. 562 + 20
18. 494 − 20
19. 737 + 200
20. 583 − 200

C

Copy and complete.

1. ☐ + 10 = 424
2. ☐ + 10 = 207
3. ☐ + 100 = 836
4. ☐ + 100 = 270

5. ☐ − 10 = 538
6. ☐ − 10 = 779
7. ☐ − 100 = 817
8. ☐ − 100 = 53

Work out

9. 2851 + 10
10. 7326 + 10
11. 5328 + 100
12. 3992 + 100

13. 5328 − 10
14. 3992 − 10
15. 8744 − 100
16. 6062 − 100

17. 4567 + 200
18. 4567 − 200
19. 4567 + 20
20. 4567 − 20

TARGET   To count in 1s, 10s and 100s from a given number.

Examples

Count on 4 from 278.

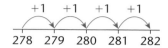

Count on 40 from 278.

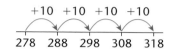

Count on 400 from 278.

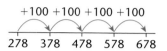

A

Count on:

1. 5 from 42
2. 7 from 85
3. 9 from 26
4. 6 from 54
5. 4 from 79
6. 8 from 63
7. 30 from 20
8. 70 from 10
9. 50 from 50
10. 40 from 37
11. 20 from 19
12. 60 from 1

Write the next four numbers in each sequence.

13. 34, 35, 36, 37
14. 93, 94, 95, 96
15. 45, 46, 47, 48
16. 30, 40, 50, 60
17. 5, 15, 25, 35
18. 28, 38, 48, 58

B

Count on:

1. 8 from 130
2. 6 from 619
3. 9 from 363
4. 7 from 886
5. 50 from 470
6. 30 from 789
7. 60 from 946
8. 80 from 567
9. 200 from 534
10. 400 from 161
11. 500 from 399
12. 300 from 617

Write the next five numbers in each sequence.

13. 172, 173, 174, 175
14. 735, 745, 755, 765
15. 208, 308, 408, 508
16. 326, 327, 328, 329
17. 564, 574, 584, 594
18. 132, 232, 332, 432

C

Count on:

1. 5 from 1578
2. 9 from 4253
3. 11 from 8419
4. 8 from 3996
5. 40 from 7562
6. 90 from 2058
7. 70 from 9283
8. 60 from 5976
9. 500 from 6672
10. 800 from 3255
11. 600 from 2938
12. 900 from 8780

Write the next five numbers in each sequence.

13. 3194, 3195, 3196, 3197
14. 7854, 7853, 7852, 7851
15. 4034, 4044, 4054, 4064
16. 9378, 9368, 9358, 9348
17. 1536, 1636, 1736, 1836
18. 6591, 6491, 6391, 6291

TARGET   To count in multiples of 4, 8, 50 and 100 from 0.

Examples

Count on five steps of 4 from 0.

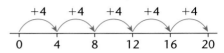

Answer *20*

Count on four steps of 8 from 0.

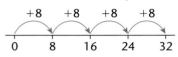

Answer *32*

A

Start at 0.
What number do you reach if you count:

1. six steps of 3
2. four steps of 5
3. seven steps of 2
4. three steps of 10
5. five steps of 2
6. nine steps of 3
7. seven steps of 10
8. six steps of 5
9. ten steps of 10
10. eight steps of 2
11. nine steps of 5
12. seven steps of 3
13. ten steps of 2
14. seven steps of 5
15. five steps of 3
16. eight steps of 10?

B

Start at 0.
What number do you reach if you count:

1. five steps of 4
2. fourteen steps of 2
3. four steps of 50
4. three steps of 8
5. six steps of 100
6. seven steps of 4
7. fifteen steps of 10
8. six steps of 50
9. six steps of 8
10. ten steps of 100
11. eleven steps of 3
12. nine steps of 50
13. nine steps of 4
14. twelve steps of 5
15. seven steps of 100
16. five steps of 8?

C

Start at 0.
What number do you reach if you count:

1. six 6s
2. four 9s
3. five 25s
4. three 7s
5. seven 9s
6. eight 6s
7. five 7s
8. ten 25s?

What number do you reach?

9. Start at 13.
Count on eight 2s.
10. Start at 24.
Count on six 5s.
11. Start at 10.
Count on five 4s.
12. Start at 15.
Count on seven 10s.
13. Start at 6.
Count on three 8s.
14. Start at 20.
Count on nine 50s.
15. Start at 11.
Count on six 3s.
16. Start at 153.
Count on four 100s.

TARGET To count in multiples of 4, 8, 50 and 100 from 0 and to give 10 or 100 more than a given number.

Examples

Count on six steps of 4 from 0.

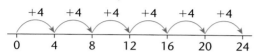

Answer *24*

Count on five steps of 10 from 271.

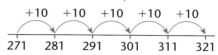

Answer *321*

A

Start at 0.
What number do you reach if you count:

1 six steps of 2

2 seven steps of 3

3 eight steps of 5

4 five steps of 10

5 eleven steps of 2

6 twelve steps of 3

7 ten steps of 5

8 nine steps of 10?

Write the first ten numbers in each sequence.

9 0 10 20 30

10 4 14 24 34

11 0 2 4 6

12 1 11 21 31

13 0 5 10 15

14 5 15 25 35

15 0 3 6 9

16 7 17 27 37

B

Start at 0.
What number do you reach if you count:

1 eight steps of 4

2 five steps of 100

3 seven steps of 8

4 seven steps of 50

5 eleven steps of 4

6 eight steps of 100

7 nine steps of 8

8 ten steps of 50?

Write the first ten numbers in each sequence.

9 0 4 8 12

10 53 63 73 83

11 0 50 100 150

12 45 145 245 345

13 0 8 16 24

14 17 117 217 317

15 0 100 200 300

16 849 859 869 879

C

What number do you reach?

1 Start at 92.
Count on five 3s.

2 Start at 465.
Count on seven 4s.

3 Start at 159.
Count on six 2s.

4 Start at 0.
Count on eight 25s.

5 Start at 28.
Count on four 6s.

6 Start at 387.
Count on five 100s.

7 Start at 37.
Count on six 9s.

8 Start at 583.
Count on eight 8s.

9 Start at 275.
Count on seven 50s.

10 Start at 44.
Count on five 8s.

11 Start at 11.
Count on six 7s.

12 Start at 1924.
Count on three 1000s.

TARGET To +/− mentally 3-digit numbers and ones.

Examples

$8 + 5 = 13$	$7 - 3 = 4$	$12 - 9 = 3$
$68 + 5 = 73$	$37 - 3 = 34$	$72 - 9 = 63$
$268 + 5 = 273$	$937 - 3 = 934$	$472 - 9 = 463$

A

Write the answers only.

1. $25 + 5$
2. $48 + 3$
3. $76 + 7$
4. $39 + 4$
5. $63 - 6$
6. $56 - 7$
7. $22 - 9$
8. $41 - 4$
9. $28 + 6$
10. $65 + 8$
11. $17 + 9$
12. $49 + 5$
13. $34 - 8$
14. $52 - 3$
15. $23 - 5$
16. $70 - 6$

Find

17. 8 more than 38
18. 6 more than 29
19. 4 less than 50
20. 7 less than 92
21. 4 more than 78
22. 9 more than 64
23. 5 less than 21
24. 9 less than 58
25. 5 more than 67
26. 7 more than 84
27. 3 less than 20
28. 8 less than 51

B

Write the answers only.

1. $268 + 7$
2. $187 + 4$
3. $653 + 9$
4. $326 + 6$
5. $107 - 8$
6. $572 - 5$
7. $453 - 9$
8. $290 - 7$
9. $257 + 8$
10. $946 + 5$
11. $788 + 6$
12. $395 + 7$
13. $145 - 6$
14. $693 - 4$
15. $214 - 7$
16. $527 - 9$

Find

17. 9 more than 342
18. 4 more than 496
19. 8 less than 562
20. 6 less than 711
21. 5 more than 198
22. 8 more than 382
23. 9 less than 400
24. 4 less than 872
25. 7 more than 359
26. 6 more than 894
27. 5 less than 544
28. 7 less than 173

C

Copy and complete.

1. $\square + 6 = 802$
2. $\square + 8 = 243$
3. $\square - 9 = 793$
4. $\square - 4 = 569$
5. $\square + 5 = 480$
6. $\square + 9 = 731$
7. $\square - 5 = 271$
8. $\square - 8 = 689$
9. $\square + 4 = 301$
10. $\square + 7 = 755$
11. $\square - 9 = 474$
12. $\square - 7 = 997$

Write the answers only.

13. $2599 + 5$
14. $7866 + 8$
15. $4281 - 6$
16. $3910 - 4$
17. $1723 + 7$
18. $6468 + 4$
19. $3841 - 5$
20. $8395 - 9$
21. $1647 + 6$
22. $5429 + 9$
23. $9861 - 7$
24. $2785 - 8$

TARGET To +/− mentally 3-digit numbers and tens.

Examples

184 + 40

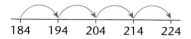

184   194   204   214   224

Answer *224*

327 − 30

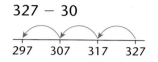

297   307   317   327

Answer *297*

A

Write the answer only.

1. 37 + 50
2. 53 + 20
3. 26 + 30
4. 41 + 50
5. 62 + 20

6. 14 + 40
7. 58 + 30
8. 32 + 60
9. 79 + 20
10. 25 + 50

11. 68 − 40
12. 97 − 80
13. 75 − 30
14. 46 − 20
15. 84 − 40

16. 51 − 20
17. 92 − 40
18. 39 − 20
19. 63 − 30
20. 85 − 60

B

Write the answer only.

1. 149 + 20
2. 404 + 30
3. 598 + 50
4. 767 + 40
5. 282 + 70

6. 923 + 40
7. 356 + 60
8. 835 + 40
9. 171 + 50
10. 619 + 70

11. 474 − 50
12. 391 − 30
13. 122 − 40
14. 658 − 60
15. 805 − 70

16. 543 − 80
17. 789 − 50
18. 916 − 30
19. 231 − 90
20. 467 − 70

C

Copy and complete.

1. 734 + ☐ = 804
2. 695 + ☐ = 755
3. 209 + ☐ = 289
4. ☐ + 30 = 977
5. ☐ + 40 = 623
6. ☐ + 50 = 411

7. 497 − ☐ = 427
8. 916 − ☐ = 876
9. 634 − ☐ = 554
10. ☐ − 60 = 113
11. ☐ − 30 = 799
12. ☐ − 90 = 245

13. 438 + ☐ = 488
14. ☐ + 60 = 441
15. 162 + ☐ = 202
16. ☐ − 70 = 603
17. 904 − ☐ = 824
18. ☐ − 70 = 259

TARGET To +/− mentally 3-digit numbers and hundreds.

Examples

451 + 300

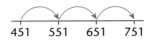

Answer *751*

451   551   651   751

926 − 400

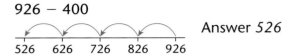

Answer *526*

526   626   726   826   926

A

Write the answer only.

1. 23 + 100
2. 68 + 100
3. 95 + 100
4. 16 + 100
5. 42 + 100

6. 100 + 72
7. 100 + 7
8. 100 + 54
9. 100 + 89
10. 100 + 33

11. 114 − 100
12. 118 − 100
13. 179 − 100
14. 197 − 100
15. 102 − 100

16. 125 − 100
17. 186 − 100
18. 161 − 100
19. 138 − 100
20. 153 − 100

B

Write the answer only.

1. 273 + 100
2. 539 + 400
3. 406 + 200
4. 151 + 300
5. 324 + 500

6. 300 + 498
7. 200 + 262
8. 100 + 515
9. 400 + 387
10. 200 + 646

11. 527 − 100
12. 774 − 500
13. 836 − 700
14. 591 − 500
15. 919 − 300

16. 456 − 100
17. 682 − 400
18. 805 − 300
19. 948 − 200
20. 364 − 300

C

Copy and complete.

1. 184 + ☐ = 984
2. 529 + ☐ = 729
3. 108 + ☐ = 608
4. ☐ + 400 = 463
5. ☐ + 500 = 955
6. ☐ + 300 = 512

7. 947 − ☐ = 347
8. 671 − ☐ = 471
9. 994 − ☐ = 594
10. ☐ − 600 = 232
11. ☐ − 600 = 126
12. ☐ − 400 = 485

13. 259 + ☐ = 959
14. ☐ + 500 = 507
15. 678 + ☐ = 878
16. ☐ − 300 = 413
17. 845 − ☐ = 545
18. ☐ − 400 = 599

TARGET   To add or subtract mentally 3-digit numbers and tens or 3-digit numbers and hundreds.

Examples

378 + 20 = 398 (70 + 20 = 90)   826 − 300 = 526 (800 − 300 = 500)

394 + 600 = 994 (300 + 600 = 900)   218 − 40 = 178 (210 − 40 = 170)

A

Work out

1. 74 + 10
2. 38 + 20
3. 46 − 10
4. 82 − 30

5. 27 + 50
6. 59 + 30
7. 65 − 20
8. 91 − 40

9. 169 + 100
10. 432 + 100
11. 387 − 100
12. 755 − 100

13. 260 + 100
14. 260 + 10
15. 520 − 100
16. 520 − 10

17. There is 220 g on a balance. Two 100 g weights are added. How much weight is on the balance?

18. A piece of string is 78 cm long. 10 cm is cut off. How much string is left?

B

Work out

1. 153 + 20
2. 436 + 50
3. 979 − 40
4. 735 − 20

5. 242 + 40
6. 518 + 60
7. 694 − 30
8. 351 − 50

9. 473 + 200
10. 362 + 400
11. 445 − 300
12. 819 − 500

13. 637 + 300
14. 284 + 500
15. 551 − 400
16. 996 − 700

17. Lisa has £264. She spends £40. How much does she have left?

18. A small box of cereal weighs 425 g. A large box weighs 300 g more. How much does the large box weigh?

C

Work out

1. 1732 + 30
2. 4417 + 40
3. 3285 − 20
4. 8649 − 40

5. 2514 + 200
6. 5037 + 500
7. 9962 − 300
8. 1658 − 500

9. 2931 + 3000
10. 5462 + 4000
11. 6507 − 6000
12. 4781 − 2000

13. 1804 + 5000
14. 6359 + 2000
15. 7263 − 4000
16. 8042 − 8000

17. There are 1472 trees in a wood. Sixty are cut down. 500 new trees are planted. How many trees are there in the wood now?

18. Darren has £537 in his bank account and £50 in cash. How much money does he have altogether?

TARGET   To use known number facts to add or subtract multiples of 10 mentally.

A

Write the answers only.

1. 3 + 5
2. 5 + 2
3. 2 + 7
4. 8 + 2
5. 4 + 3
6. 7 + 3
7. 3 + 6
8. 6 + 4

9. 7 − 2
10. 10 − 4
11. 8 − 4
12. 10 − 2
13. 9 − 6
14. 10 − 5
15. 8 − 2
16. 9 − 5

17. 50 + 30
18. 70 + 20
19. 60 + 30
20. 40 + 50
21. 20 + 60
22. 50 + 40
23. 40 + 60
24. 30 + 40

25. 100 − 60
26. 90 − 40
27. 80 − 50
28. 100 − 80
29. 90 − 30
30. 70 − 40
31. 100 − 30
32. 80 − 60

33. Copy and complete using the three given numbers only.

7 + 9 = 16

☐ + ☐ = 16

☐ − ☐ = 7

☐ − ☐ = 9

B

Write the answers only.

1. 6 + 8
2. 9 + 6
3. 5 + 9
4. 8 + 7
5. 7 + 8
6. 10 + 6
7. 8 + 9
8. 9 + 7

9. 17 − 9
10. 20 − 6
11. 19 − 13
12. 16 − 8
13. 20 − 12
14. 18 − 9
15. 15 − 8
16. 19 − 7

17. 80 + 60
18. 50 + 70
19. 70 + 90
20. 90 + 80
21. 60 + 90
22. 80 + 80
23. 90 + 90
24. 70 + 60

25. 150 − 60
26. 180 − 120
27. 170 − 80
28. 200 − 90
29. 190 − 80
30. 160 − 70
31. 140 − 60
32. 200 − 130

For each fact write three other facts.

33. 42 + 25 = 67
34. 81 − 44 = 37
35. 56 + 38 = 94
36. 76 − 49 = 27

C

Copy and complete.

1. 80 + ☐ = 170
2. 90 + ☐ = 130
3. ☐ + 50 = 120
4. ☐ + 80 = 140

5. 170 − ☐ = 80
6. 200 − ☐ = 140
7. ☐ − 80 = 80
8. ☐ − 70 = 120

9. 50 + ☐ = 140
10. 80 + ☐ = 150
11. ☐ + 90 = 180
12. ☐ + 70 = 140

13. 170 − ☐ = 60
14. 200 − ☐ = 120
15. ☐ − 70 = 110
16. ☐ − 130 = 60

Use the three numbers given to write four number facts.

17. 88, 25, 63
18. 27, 49, 76
19. 56, 92, 36
20. 22, 100, 78
21. 243, 60, 303
22. 1000, 550, 450

TARGET To use known number facts to add or subtract mentally multiples of 10 or 100.

Example 1
5 + 9 = 14
50 + 90 = 140
500 + 900 = 1400

Example 2
10 − 4 = 6
100 − 40 = 60
1000 − 400 = 600

Example 3
Double 4 = 8
Double 40 = 80
Double 400 = 800

A

Copy and complete as in Example 1.

1 2 + 5 = 7
20 + ☐ = ☐
200 + ☐ = ☐

2 6 + 3 = 9
☐ + ☐ = 90
☐ + ☐ = 900

3 8 − 3 = 5
80 − ☐ = ☐
800 − ☐ = ☐

4 9 − 7 = 2
☐ − ☐ = 20
☐ − ☐ = 200

What needs to be added to each number to make 10?

5 4   **9** 6
6 7   **10** 3
7 2   **11** 8
8 9   **12** 1

Double

13 5   **17** 4
14 8   **18** 6
15 2   **19** 9
16 7   **20** 3

B

Copy and complete.

1 90 + ☐ = 130
2 70 + ☐ = 150
3 80 + ☐ = 140
4 50 + ☐ = 120

5 300 + ☐ = 800
6 600 + ☐ = 900
7 200 + ☐ = 700
8 500 + ☐ = 900

9 130 − ☐ = 60
10 160 − ☐ = 70
11 120 − ☐ = 80
12 140 − ☐ = 90

What needs to be added to each number to make 100?

13 40   **17** 10
14 80   **18** 60
15 30   **19** 20
16 50   **20** 70

Double

21 30   **25** 20
22 60   **26** 70
23 80   **27** 40
24 50   **28** 90

C

Copy and complete.

1 320 + ☐ = 500
2 540 + ☐ = 910
3 430 + ☐ = 680
4 380 + ☐ = 700

5 410 − ☐ = 250
6 590 − ☐ = 370
7 870 − ☐ = 530
8 640 − ☐ = 460

9 100 − ☐ = 85
10 100 − ☐ = 25
11 100 − ☐ = 65
12 100 − ☐ = 5

13 1000 − ☐ = 50
14 1000 − ☐ = 750
15 1000 − ☐ = 150
16 1000 − ☐ = 350

Double

17 15   **23** 56
18 75   **24** 35
19 45   **25** 84
20 650   **26** 280
21 250   **27** 950
22 850   **28** 730

TARGET To +/− multiples of 10 and find pairs of numbers that make 100 and use them in calculations.

Examples

13 − 7 = 6   100 = 58 + ☐   58 → 60   2   115 − 58   58 → 60   2

130 − 70 = 60   60 → 100 $\underline{40}$ 60 → 100   40

                            Answer $\overline{42}$ 100 → 115 $\underline{15}$

                                                 Answer $\overline{57}$

A

1. 6 + 8
2. 9 + 4
3. 7 + 6
4. 5 + 7
5. 8 + 9
6. 11 + 7
7. 6 + 9
8. 13 + 6
9. 9 + 7
10. 12 + 5
11. 8 + 6
12. 7 + 8
13. 13 − 5
14. 16 − 7
15. 12 − 8
16. 15 − 6
17. 17 − 9
18. 14 − 7
19. 20 − 11
20. 19 − 12
21. 11 − 6
22. 14 − 9
23. 20 − 7
24. 18 − 9

B

Write the answers only.

1. 90 + 60
2. 70 + 90
3. 80 + 50
4. 60 + 70
5. 90 + 80
6. 80 + 70
7. 120 − 50
8. 140 − 80
9. 200 − 120
10. 160 − 80
11. 130 − 90
12. 150 − 70

What needs to be added to each number to make 100?

13. 75
14. 35
15. 85
16. 5
17. 55
18. 25
19. 46
20. 92
21. 27
22. 64
23. 11
24. 73

Work out

25. 105 − 82
26. 113 − 77
27. 136 − 95
28. 121 − 83
29. 118 − 91
30. 144 − 78
31. 102 − 66
32. 127 − 98
33. 135 − 76
34. 116 − 89
35. 104 − 42
36. 143 − 94
37. 129 − 79
38. 132 − 83
39. 158 − 97
40. 111 − 55

C

What needs to be added to each number to make 1000?

1. 650
2. 150
3. 950
4. 450
5. 250
6. 850
7. 380
8. 730
9. 160
10. 20
11. 810
12. 540

Copy and complete.

13. 800 + ☐ = 1500
14. 700 + ☐ = 1600
15. 900 + ☐ = 1400
16. 600 + ☐ = 1300
17. 1300 − ☐ = 400
18. 1500 − ☐ = 900
19. 1700 − ☐ = 800
20. 1400 − ☐ = 600
21. 324 − ☐ = 286
22. 217 − ☐ = 152
23. 202 − ☐ = 69
24. 238 − ☐ = 171
25. 345 − ☐ = 295
26. 229 − ☐ = 164
27. 353 − ☐ = 278
28. 216 − ☐ = 83

TARGET To +/− mentally 3-digit numbers and multiples or near multiples of 10 or 100.

Examples

518 + 206 = 518 + 200 + 6
          = 718 + 6
          = 724

518 + 198 = 518 + 200 − 2
          = 718 − 2
          = 716

963 − 41 = 963 − 40 − 1
         = 923 − 1
         = 922

963 − 38 = 963 − 40 + 2
         = 923 + 2
         = 925

A

Work out

1. 33 + 10
2. 59 + 10
3. 61 − 10
4. 76 − 10

5. 42 + 10
6. 42 + 11
7. 67 − 10
8. 67 − 9

9. 58 + 20
10. 58 + 19
11. 84 − 20
12. 84 − 21

13. 46 + 9
14. 63 + 21
15. 97 − 11
16. 75 − 19

Work out

17. 230 + 100
18. 593 + 100
19. 346 − 100
20. 762 − 100

21. 418 + 100
22. 418 + 99
23. 675 − 100
24. 675 − 101

25. 524 + 101
26. 850 − 99
27. 189 + 99
28. 707 − 101

B

Work out

1. 35 + 30
2. 342 + 50
3. 79 − 60
4. 293 − 40

5. 162 + 300
6. 540 + 400
7. 617 − 200
8. 874 − 600

9. 42 + 30
10. 42 + 29
11. 956 − 400
12. 956 − 403

13. 83 − 50
14. 83 − 51
15. 365 + 400
16. 365 + 398

Work out

17. £745 + £52
18. £527 + £305
19. £274 − £39
20. £838 − £497

C

Work out

1. 1325 + 30
2. 1558 + 70
3. 3962 − 40
4. 2439 − 60

5. 1268 + 500
6. 3847 + 400
7. 2750 − 300
8. 6214 − 700

Copy and complete.

9. 317 + ☐ = 358
10. 783 − ☐ = 734
11. ☐ + 298 = 824
12. ☐ − 203 = 262

13. 147 + ☐ = 176
14. 984 − ☐ = 923
15. ☐ + 504 = 1135
16. ☐ − 396 = 1028

Work out

17. £14·28 + 39p
18. £23·75 − £5·02
19. 1756 km + 598 km
20. 2183 km − 304 km

TARGET To use different strategies to +/− mentally one-digit numbers to or from 2-digit numbers.

Examples

BRIDGING

$75 − 8 = 67$

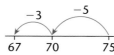

START WITH LARGEST

Add 7, 8, 19 and 4

$19 + 8 + 7 + 4$

$27 + 7 + 4$

$34 + 4$

38

MAKE 10

$5 + 7 + 8 + 3$

$10 + 8 + 5$

$18 + 5$

23

$4 + 9 + 7 + 6$

$10 + 9 + 7$

$19 + 7$

26

A

Work out by bridging.

1. $7 + 6$
2. $8 + 4$
3. $9 + 7$
4. $6 + 8$

5. $15 + 6$
6. $18 + 7$
7. $17 + 9$
8. $19 + 5$

9. $16 − 9$
10. $13 − 8$
11. $15 − 6$
12. $12 − 5$

13. $24 − 7$
14. $23 − 5$
15. $21 − 9$
16. $26 − 7$

Work out

17. $8 + 25$
18. $6 + 46$
19. $5 + 38$
20. $7 + 54$

21. $9 + 68$
22. $4 + 27$
23. $8 + 46$
24. $6 + 39$

Find the totals.

25. $9 + 8 + 1$
26. $5 + 6 + 5$
27. $6 + 9 + 4$
28. $5 + 3 + 7$
29. $2 + 7 + 8$
30. $3 + 15 + 5$

B

Work out by bridging.

1. $56 + 7$
2. $48 + 4$
3. $95 + 9$
4. $73 + 8$

5. $87 + 6$
6. $59 + 7$
7. $34 + 8$
8. $68 + 6$

9. $75 − 8$
10. $53 − 5$
11. $81 − 7$
12. $38 − 9$

13. $96 − 9$
14. $44 − 8$
15. $67 − 9$
16. $72 − 6$

Copy and complete.

17. $5 + 3 + 26 = \square$
18. $4 + 38 + \square = 49$
19. $\square + 23 + 6 = 37$
20. $9 + \square + 35 = 48$

Copy and complete.

21. $4 + 9 + 6 + 2 = \square$
22. $\square + 3 + 5 + 7 = 21$
23. $5 + \square + 8 + 5 = 25$
24. $6 + 8 + \square + 12 = 39$
25. $11 + 2 + 9 + 5 = \square$
26. $6 + \square + 17 + 3 = 30$

C

Copy and complete.

1. $97 + \square = 105$
2. $95 + \square = 102$
3. $98 + \square = 104$
4. $92 + \square = 101$

5. $43 − \square = 26$
6. $76 − \square = 52$
7. $82 − \square = 47$
8. $65 − \square = 32$

Add up each set of numbers.

9. 15, 9, 36, 8
10. 8, 55, 17, 6
11. 7, 14, 5, 29
12. 4, 9, 48, 13
13. 6, 37, 19, 5
14. 20, 30, 60, 70
15. 50, 30, 40, 50
16. 80, 50, 20, 40
17. 60, 10, 80, 90
18. 40, 70, 50, 60

TARGET   To add or subtract mentally one-digit numbers to or from 2-digit numbers.

Examples

COUNTING
39 − 4

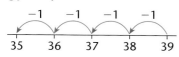

Answer *35*

BRIDGING
57 + 9

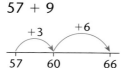

Answer *66*

PARTITIONING

78 + 5	94 − 8
70 + 8 + 5	80 + 14 − 8
70 + 13	80 + 6
80 + 3	
Answer *83*	Answer *86*

A

Work out by counting.

1 13 + 4   5 28 − 5

2 21 + 5   6 26 − 4

3 15 + 3   7 39 − 7

4 32 + 6   8 37 − 6

Work out by bridging.

9 19 + 3   13 22 − 6

10 15 + 6   14 24 − 5

11 28 + 7   15 31 − 4

12 26 + 5   16 33 − 8

Find

17 7 less than 22

18 6 less than 23

19 8 less than 24

20 5 less than 21

Find

21 4 more than 19

22 6 more than 17

23 9 more than 13

24 7 more than 18

B

Work out

1 49 + 5   5 62 − 4

2 67 + 8   6 83 − 7

3 85 + 7   7 54 − 6

4 38 + 6   8 71 − 8

Find

9 8 more than 86

10 5 less than 63

11 6 more than 57

12 7 less than 41

13 7 more than 68

14 9 less than 94

Copy and complete the squares.

15

+	8	6	9
35		41	
68			
86			95

16

−	5	9	7
52			45
84			
61	56		

C

Work out

1 158 + 6

2 347 + 4

3 442 − 5

4 286 − 9

5 304 + 8

6 169 + 5

7 552 − 7

8 261 − 4

9 433 + 9

10 177 + 7

11 693 − 8

12 372 − 6

Copy and complete the squares.

13

+	5	9	7
247			
529			
856			

14

−	9	6	8
743			
475			
902			

TARGET   To develop strategies to add or subtract mentally.

Examples

+/− MULTIPLES OF 10
$58 + 30 = 88$
$158 + 30 = 188$

$62 − 40 = 22$
$162 − 40 = 122$

+/− NEAR MULTIPLES OF 10
$58 + 19 = 58 + 20 − 1$
$\qquad = 78 − 1$
$\qquad = 77$

$95 − 29 = 95 − 30 + 1$
$\qquad = 65 + 1$
$\qquad = 64$

ADDING NEAR DOUBLES
$25 + 26 = $ Double $25 + 1$
$\qquad = 50 + 1$
$\qquad = 51$

$22 + 19 = $ Double $20 + 2 − 1$
$\qquad = 40 + 1$
$\qquad = 41$

A

Work out

1. $35 + 10$
2. $57 + 10$
3. $82 + 10$
4. $64 + 10$
5. $29 + 10$
6. $43 + 10$
7. $66 − 10$
8. $49 − 10$
9. $93 − 10$
10. $32 − 10$
11. $74 − 10$
12. $51 − 10$

13. $76 + 9$
14. $14 + 11$
15. $58 + 9$
16. $37 + 11$
17. $63 + 9$
18. $85 + 11$
19. $87 − 9$
20. $45 − 11$
21. $38 − 9$
22. $96 − 11$
23. $54 − 9$
24. $73 − 11$

25. $12 + 11$
26. $6 + 7$
27. $13 + 12$
28. $20 + 21$
29. $14 + 15$
30. $9 + 8$
31. $10 + 11$
32. $6 + 5$
33. $40 + 38$
34. $8 + 7$
35. $13 + 14$
36. $30 + 32$

B

Work out

1. $48 + 30$
2. $21 + 20$
3. $52 + 40$
4. $84 + 50$
5. $97 + 30$
6. $75 + 40$
7. $86 − 30$
8. $95 − 20$
9. $67 − 40$
10. $114 − 30$
11. $146 − 50$
12. $129 − 60$

13. $36 + 19$
14. $62 + 29$
15. $93 + 19$
16. $42 + 31$
17. $78 + 21$
18. $56 + 31$
19. $54 − 29$
20. $72 − 19$
21. $98 − 29$
22. $65 − 21$
23. $46 − 31$
24. $89 − 21$

25. $18 + 19$
26. $60 + 50$
27. $35 + 37$
28. $19 + 17$
29. $70 + 80$
30. $45 + 44$
31. $60 + 70$
32. $17 + 16$
33. $25 + 23$
34. $90 + 80$
35. $16 + 18$
36. $55 + 56$

C

Copy and complete.

1. $352 + \square = 412$
2. $795 + \square = 875$
3. $279 + \square = 329$
4. $536 − \square = 466$
5. $824 − \square = 784$
6. $447 − \square = 357$

7. $\square + 39 = 94$
8. $\square − 49 = 63$
9. $\square + 51 = 125$
10. $\square − 41 = 79$
11. $\square + 58 = 141$
12. $\square − 62 = 66$

13. $360 + 350 = \square$
14. $270 + 280 = \square$
15. $490 + 470 = \square$
16. $380 + 390 = \square$
17. $260 + 280 = \square$
18. $470 + 450 = \square$

TARGET To use partitioning to add or subtract numbers mentally.

Examples

$$57 + 26 = 57 + 20 + 6$$
$$= 77 + 6$$
$$= 83$$

$$112 - 55 = 112 - 50 - 5$$
$$= 62 - 5$$
$$= 57$$

A
Work out

1 12 + 15
2 17 + 21
3 18 + 13
4 23 + 12

5 14 + 26
6 15 + 19
7 21 + 14
8 16 + 17

9 28 − 13
10 32 − 16
11 27 − 12
12 36 − 24

13 34 − 17
14 29 − 15
15 31 − 19
16 39 − 25

B
Work out

1 37 + 17
2 45 + 29
3 39 + 23
4 56 + 35
5 48 + 16
6 64 + 28
7 77 + 54
8 54 + 47
9 93 + 45
10 86 + 38

11 78 − 24
12 95 − 67
13 66 − 23
14 53 − 38
15 89 − 52
16 117 − 45
17 142 − 66
18 125 − 39
19 106 − 47
20 151 − 74

C
Copy and complete.

1 67 + ☐ = 83
2 86 + ☐ = 115
3 38 + ☐ = 72
4 53 + ☐ = 121
5 49 + ☐ = 94
6 88 − ☐ = 37
7 65 − ☐ = 26
8 97 − ☐ = 58
9 59 − ☐ = 15
10 76 − ☐ = 49

TARGET To use counting up to subtract numbers mentally.

Examples

$65 - 38$

$38 \rightarrow 40$	2
$40 \rightarrow 60$	20
$60 \rightarrow 65$	5
Answer	27

$112 - 55$

$55 \rightarrow 60$	5
$60 \rightarrow 110$	50
$110 \rightarrow 112$	2
Answer	57

A
Count up from:

1 26 to 33
2 37 to 42
3 52 to 61
4 29 to 33
5 98 to 105
6 81 to 96
7 65 to 73
8 43 to 59
9 54 to 78
10 26 to 44.

B
Count up to work out.

1 30 − 13
2 40 − 19
3 70 − 24
4 50 − 35
5 90 − 52
6 81 − 58
7 65 − 46
8 93 − 38
9 54 − 27
10 72 − 56

11 100 − 68
12 120 − 55
13 110 − 86
14 140 − 91
15 130 − 77
16 121 − 34
17 156 − 88
18 103 − 57
19 132 − 39
20 115 − 76

C
Copy and complete.

1 146 − ☐ = 72
2 171 − ☐ = 57
3 165 − ☐ = 89
4 182 − ☐ = 48
5 153 − ☐ = 66
6 322 − ☐ = 245
7 603 − ☐ = 518
8 947 − ☐ = 883
9 576 − ☐ = 369
10 834 − ☐ = 478

TARGET To add numbers with up to 3 digits.

Examples

```
  H  T  U
  2  3  6       6 + 7 = 13
+ 1  4  7       3 in units (3)
  3  8  3       10 is carried into 10s (¹)
     1
```

```
  H  T  U
  5  7  3       70 + 80 = 150
+ 2  8  4       50 in 10s (5)
  8  5  7       100 is carried into 100s (¹)
     1
```

A

Copy and complete.

1 35
    + 23

2 43
    + 22

3 56
    + 31

4 32
    + 27

5 61
    + 35

6 47
    + 21

7 59
    + 30

8 44
    + 34

9 72
    + 26

10 55
     + 24

11 A football club has 27 junior players and 53 adult players. How many people play at the club?

12 A bicycle shop has 48 bikes for sale and 33 being repaired. How many bikes are in the shop altogether?

B

Copy and complete.

1 46
    + 37

2 49
    + 43

3 53
    + 27

4 84
    + 55

5 67
    + 41

6 175
    + 119

7 246
    + 135

8 484
    + 243

9 317
    + 257

10 591
     + 358

11 A farmer has 276 sheep. 139 lambs are born in the spring. How many sheep are there now on the farm?

12 Micky has read 67 pages of his book. He still has 143 pages to read. How many pages are there in his book?

13 A basketball team win their match 88 points to 73. How many points were scored in the game altogether?

C

Set out as in the example.

1 148 + 157

2 285 + 167

3 457 + 249

4 1389 + 336

5 2454 + 376

6 1596 + 1348

7 2378 + 1259

8 3463 + 2188

9 6559 + 2264

10 4387 + 3178

11 Henry is paid £2749 every month. His pay goes up by £285. What is he paid now?

12 A store has 2684 customers during the week and a further 1937 at the weekend. How many customers does the store have in the whole week altogether?

13 In one day 5492 vehicles cross a bridge going north and 3828 cross it going south. How many vehicles cross the bridge altogether?

TARGET **To practise adding 3-digit numbers.**

Examples

```
  H T U
  3 1 6        6 + 8 = 14
+ 2 5 8        4 in units (4)
  5 7 4        10 is carried into 10s (¹)
    1
```

```
  H T U
  6 4 0        40 + 90 = 130
+ 1 9 3        30 in 10s (3)
  8 3 3        100 is carried into 100s (¹)
    1
```

A

Copy and complete.

1.  ```
       34
     + 25
    ```
2.  ```
       43
     + 26
    ```
3.  ```
       45
     + 32
    ```
4.  ```
       36
     + 31
    ```
5.  ```
       53
     + 24
    ```
6.  ```
       63
     + 38
    ```
7.  ```
       59
     + 42
    ```
8.  ```
       76
     + 34
    ```
9.  ```
       68
     + 26
    ```
10. ```
       54
     + 39
    ```

11. Dale is 48. Sam is 27 years older. How old is Sam?

12. There are 42 boys and 39 girls in Year 3. How many children are there in Year 3 altogether?

13. Jenny has 38 1st class stamps and 54 2nd class stamps. How many stamps does she have altogether?

B

Copy and complete.

1.  ```
        274
     + 127
    ```
2.  ```
        355
     + 138
    ```
3.  ```
        482
     + 144
    ```
4.  ```
        369
     + 215
    ```
5.  ```
        593
     + 246
    ```
6.  ```
        258
     + 243
    ```
7.  ```
        586
     + 357
    ```
8.  ```
        397
     + 336
    ```
9.  ```
        679
     + 141
    ```
10. ```
        465
     + 347
    ```

11. Salma drives 176 km in the morning and 145 km later in the day. How far has she travelled altogether?

12. A junior school has 234 pupils. A secondary school has 419 more pupils than the junior school. How many children go to the secondary school?

C

Set out as in the example.

1. 2463 + 1725
2. 2278 + 2493
3. 5934 + 1628
4. 3375 + 2459
5. 4516 + 2535
6. 6438 + 2292
7. 3822 + 3895
8. 5464 + 2196
9. 8547 + 1258
10. 4376 + 1836

11. In one year a factory produces 7596 cars. The next year production goes up by 1438. How many cars are made in the second year?

12.

The air distance from London to Hong Kong is 5979 miles. The flight to Honolulu is 1273 miles further. How long is the flight from London to Honolulu?

TARGET   To subtract numbers with up to 3 digits.

If the digit in the top row is smaller than the digit below it, borrow 10 from the column to the left.

Examples

```
  H  T  U
        6  1
     8  7̸  2          2 − 8
   − 1  5  8          Borrow 10 from 70 (7̸, 2)
     7  1  4          12 − 8 = 4
```

```
  H  T  U
     5  1
     6̸  1  8          10 − 50
   − 3  5  6          Borrow 100 from 600 (6̸, 1)
     2  6  2          110 − 50 = 60
```

A

Copy and complete.

1	48 − 12	**6**	99 − 40
2	76 − 34	**7**	58 − 26
3	57 − 23	**8**	95 − 71
4	85 − 45	**9**	65 − 24
5	64 − 32	**10**	78 − 53

11 There are 68 passengers on a bus. 35 are upstairs. How many passengers are downstairs?

12 Omar has 96p. He spends 55p. How much does he have left?

13 There are 52 complete weeks in a year. 21 have passed before Paula's birthday. How many weeks is it to the end of the year?

B

Copy and complete.

1	65 − 49	**6**	364 − 207
2	81 − 52	**7**	781 − 546
3	92 − 35	**8**	297 − 149
4	80 − 37	**9**	823 − 273
5	73 − 46	**10**	954 − 716

11 Four coaches carry 240 children altogether. 126 children travel on the first two coaches. How many are on the last two coaches?

12 A shop has 325 customers on Monday and 87 fewer on Tuesday. How many customers does the shop have on Tuesday?

13 A newsagent has 750 newspapers. 463 are delivered to people's homes. How many are on sale in the shop?

C

Copy and complete.

1	2837 − 1562	**6**	6915 − 2319
2	3764 − 1813	**7**	7463 − 4593
3	4892 − 2954	**8**	4736 − 1347
4	5526 − 1294	**9**	9282 − 7690
5	8358 − 3851	**10**	8505 − 2783

11 A trawler catches 1326 fish in one net and 718 fewer in a second net. How many fish are caught in the second net?

12 There are 6863 entries to a competition. 2147 have the right answers. How many of the competition entries have wrong answers?

TARGET To practise subtracting 3-digit numbers.

If the digit in the top row is smaller than the digit below it, borrow 10 from the column to the left.

Examples

```
  H T U
      6 1
  4 7 0        0 – 2
– 1 4 2        Borrow 10 from 70 (7, 0)
  2 2 8        10 – 2 = 8
```

```
  H T U
    7 1
  8 3 5        30 – 80
– 4 8 1        Borrow 100 from 800 (8, 3)
  3 5 4        130 – 80 = 50
```

A

Copy and complete.

1) 77
  – 34

2) 68
  – 43

3) 55
  – 21

4) 89
  – 37

5) 96
  – 53

6) 86
  – 68

7) 54
  – 39

8) 92
  – 77

9) 60
  – 24

10) 75
  – 46

11) There are 64 tents in a campsite. 27 tents are taken down. How many tents are still up in the campsite?

12) Jarad's book has 75 pages. He has 39 left. How many pages has he read?

13) Ed has 92 drawing pins. He uses 48. How many does he have left?

B

Copy and complete.

1) 347
  – 164

2) 673
  – 217

3) 526
  – 353

4) 495
  – 128

5) 358
  – 276

6) 612
  – 347

7) 564
  – 278

8) 813
  – 685

9) 930
  – 694

10) 751
  – 259

11) A florist has 240 bunches of flowers. At the end of the day 117 are left. How many have been sold?

12) A hotel has 238 rooms. 196 have people staying in them. How many rooms are empty?

13) There are 153 children on the playground and 78 in the canteen having lunch. How many more children are on the playground than in the canteen?

C

Copy and complete.

1) 2579
  – 1823

2) 6938
  – 3675

3) 5260
  – 2413

4) 3842
  – 1287

5) 8195
  – 3649

6) 4324
  – 2695

7) 7361
  – 1963

8) 6513
  – 4785

9) 9420
  – 5758

10) 5016
  – 3479

11) When 3163 Martians were asked to choose their favourite TV programme, 2584 chose Dr Who. How many chose a different programme?

12) Rosie has £9420 in her bank account. She takes out £1752. How much is left in the account?

TARGET   To estimate the answer to +/− before working out.

Examples

Estimate answers first

584 →	5 8 0	(58 tens)
+236 → +	2 3 0	(23 tens)
	8 1 0	(81 tens)
	1	

Work out

```
  5 8 4
+ 2 3 6
  8 2 0
  1 1
```

Answer is slightly larger than 810.

Estimate answer first

639 →	6 3 0	(63 tens)
−475 → −	4 7 0	(47 tens)
	1 6 0	(16 tens)

Work out

```
  ⁵6̶ ¹3 9
− 4 7 5
  1 6 4
```

Answer is approximately 160.

A

Estimate the answer before working out.

1   27
    + 25

2   34
    + 29

3   56
    + 34

4   45
    + 37

5   39
    + 36

6   68
    + 23

7   59
    − 37

8   86
    − 52

9   64
    − 43

10   93
    − 28

11   71
    − 49

12   84
    − 67

13 There are 85 fish in a pond. 36 are added. How many fish are in the pond?

14 Geoff has 65p. He spends 29p. How much does he have left?

B

Estimate the answer before working out.

1   483
    + 224

2   246
    + 157

3   372
    + 195

4   525
    + 286

5   691
    + 147

6   439
    + 478

7   318
    − 142

8   760
    − 235

9   249
    − 153

10   576
    − 297

11   824
    − 469

12   651
    − 383

13 Maria pays £169 for her flight to Spain and £479 for a week at a hotel. How much more has she spent on her hotel than on her flight?

14 In one day a leisure centre is used by 248 adults and 155 children. How many people used the centre altogether?

C

Estimate the answer before working out.

1   8163
    + 1458

2   4817
    + 3647

3   2354
    + 1586

4   6675
    + 1863

5   3409
    + 3292

6   5748
    + 1387

7   2433
    − 815

8   6852
    − 5379

9   9305
    − 5743

10   3617
    − 2158

11   5941
    − 4946

12   7504
    − 5986

13 A shop has takings of £5836 on Saturday and £3178 on Sunday. What are the total takings for the weekend?

14 A library has 4261 books. 1597 are out on loan. How many books are on the shelves?

TARGET　To use the inverse operation to check answers to +/−.

Examples

```
    4 6 9        Reverse      6 11 1                          6 1          Reverse       1 2 7
  + 2 5 7        order to     7̶ 2̶ 6                        2 7̶ 2         order to     + 1 4 5
    ─────        check       − 2 5 7                      − 1 4 5         check         ─────
    7 2 6                     ─────                        ─────                        2 7 2
    1 1                       4 6 9                        1 2 7                          1
```

A

Work out and then check with inverse operation.

1　49　　　**7**　48
　+ 23　　　　− 21

2　55　　　**8**　91
　+ 36　　　　− 37

3　63　　　**9**　75
　+ 18　　　　− 46

4　37　　**10**　53
　+ 29　　　　− 38

5　46　　**11**　60
　+ 34　　　　− 42

6　28　　**12**　62
　+ 25　　　　− 35

13 There are 39 people on the top deck of a bus and 35 on the lower deck. How many people are on the bus altogether?

B

Work out and then check with inverse operation.

1　328　　　**7**　274
　+ 242　　　　− 156

2　264　　　**8**　569
　+　95　　　　− 282

3　457　　　**9**　352
　+ 336　　　　− 117

4　715　　**10**　608
　+ 178　　　　− 245

5　539　　**11**　941
　+ 445　　　　− 493

6　386　　**12**　835
　+ 197　　　　− 560

13 There are 217 houses on one side of the road and 194 on the other side. How many houses are there on the road altogether?

14 A school has 343 pupils. 185 have a school dinner. How many children do not have a school dinner?

C

Work out and then check with inverse operation.

1　1295　　　**7**　2582
　+　472　　　　−　934

2　3607　　　**8**　4308
　+ 2598　　　　− 2358

3　6382　　　**9**　7614
　+ 2645　　　　− 1527

4　2728　　**10**　9276
　+　476　　　　− 5839

5　4544　　**11**　8593
　+ 3783　　　　− 3759

6　5819　　**12**　6840
　+ 1394　　　　− 3457

13 A flock of 5647 starlings is joined by a flock of 2893. How many starlings are there in the combined flocks?

14 A library has 7350 books. 2542 are out on loan. How many books are on the library shelves?

TARGET   To solve missing number problems involving +/−.

Examples $35 + \square = 63$ $\square - 40 = 324$

$63 - 35 = 28$ $324 + 40 = 364$

Missing number is 28.   Missing number is 364.

A

Copy and complete.

1. $7 + \square = 20$
2. $15 + \square = 20$
3. $20 - \square = 12$
4. $20 - \square = 4$

5. $\square + 8 = 55$
6. $\square + 5 = 31$
7. $\square - 6 = 57$
8. $\square - 9 = 84$

9. $16 + \square = 29$
10. $19 + \square = 35$
11. $28 - \square = 11$
12. $31 - \square = 17$

13. $\square + 20 = 62$
14. $\square + 50 = 85$
15. $\square - 40 = 79$
16. $\square - 30 = 41$

17. $15 + \square = 32$
18. $17 + \square = 38$
19. $26 - \square = 12$
20. $34 - \square = 19$

21. $\square + 100 = 539$
22. $\square + 100 = 245$
23. $\square - 100 = 481$
24. $\square - 100 = 173$

B

Copy and complete.

1. $29 + \square = 100$
2. $73 + \square = 100$
3. $100 - \square = 56$
4. $100 - \square = 8$

5. $\square + 7 = 342$
6. $\square + 9 = 178$
7. $\square - 4 = 519$
8. $\square - 8 = 893$

9. $38 + \square = 72$
10. $65 + \square = 114$
11. $83 - \square = 47$
12. $124 - \square = 59$

13. $\square + 30 = 653$
14. $\square + 40 = 198$
15. $\square - 60 = 917$
16. $\square - 20 = 264$

17. $59 + \square = 85$
18. $34 + \square = 113$
19. $95 - \square = 28$
20. $132 - \square = 59$

21. $\square + 200 = 726$
22. $\square + 400 = 843$
23. $\square - 600 = 108$
24. $\square - 900 = 35$

C

Copy and complete.

1. $310 + \square = 1000$
2. $850 + \square = 1000$
3. $1000 - \square = 620$
4. $1000 - \square = 970$

5. $\square + 6 = 1482$
6. $\square + 8 = 3207$
7. $\square - 9 = 9726$
8. $\square - 5 = 4647$

9. $64 + \square = 301$
10. $37 + \square = 925$
11. $742 - \square = 68$
12. $515 - \square = 56$

13. $\square + 70 = 2316$
14. $\square + 60 = 4744$
15. $\square - 50 = 7082$
16. $\square - 80 = 1658$

17. $96 + \square = 741$
18. $38 + \square = 216$
19. $461 - \square = 85$
20. $824 - \square = 67$

21. $\square + 700 = 3159$
22. $\square + 500 = 8303$
23. $\square - 800 = 2475$
24. $\square - 600 = 6912$

TARGET To solve word problems using written methods for +/−.

A Post Office sells 537 1st class stamps and 285 2nd class stamps.

1 How many stamps are sold altogether?

2 How many more 1st class stamps are sold than 2nd class stamps?

```
1      5 3 7        2    ⁴5̶ ¹3 7
     + 2 8 5           − 2 8 5
       8 2 2             2 5 2
       1 1
```

Answers 1 *822* stamps are sold altogether.

2 *252* more 1st class stamps are sold than 2nd class stamps.

A

1 There are 28 children in 3F and 29 in 3W. How many children are there in the two Year 3 classes altogether?

2 Sixty-three people are in one coach of a train. 27 get off at a station. How many passengers are left in the coach?

3 A flower bed has 56 yellow flowers and 34 red flowers. How many flowers are there in the display altogether?

4 In all of their matches a football team scores 71 goals and has 52 scored against them. How many more goals do they score than let in?

5 There are 35 more black and white cows in a field than there are brown cows. There are 47 brown cows in the field. How many black and white cows are there?

6 Nick has 92p. He spends 39p. How much does he have left?

B

1 A shop has 460 newspapers for sale. 418 are sold. How many papers have not been sold?

2 The afternoon performance of the School Concert is watched by 165 people. The evening performance is watched by 193 people. How many people see the two performances altogether?

3 A factory employs 346 men. 227 more women work at the factory than men. How many women work at the factory?

4 A school has 358 pupils. During a school year 129 pupils do not have a single absence. How many pupils have had at least one absence?

5 A dairy produces 458 large bottles of milk and 343 small bottles. How many bottles of milk are produced altogether?

C

1 Walter has £5836 in his savings account. He pays in a further £1659. How much does he now have in his account?

2 There are 2813 spaces in the city centre car parks. 1684 have been taken. How many spaces are available for parking?

3 At the start of the year a forest has 6715 trees. During the year 835 more trees are planted than are cut down. How many trees are there in the forest at the end of the year?

4 Cartford has 9256 people living in the town. 7281 live to the north of the River Cart. How many people live to the south of the river?

5 A total of 6074 people visit a zoo. 2309 are children. How many of the visitors are adults?

TARGET   To solve number puzzles involving addition and subtraction.

In an addition pyramid, pairs of numbers
are added to make the number above them.

Example

```
        30
      ↗  ↖
    19    11
   ↗ ↖   ↗ ↖
  12   7    4
```

Copy and complete the following addition pyramids.

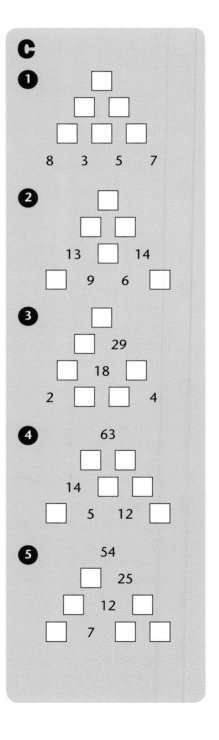

A

1.
```
    □
  □   □
 2  3  6
```

2.
```
    □
  □   □
 1  5  7
```

3.
```
    □
  □   □
 6  7  0
```

4.
```
    □
  □     8
 4  5    □
```

5.
```
    □
 12    □
 8   □   3
```

6.
```
    □
 10    □
  □  9  4
```

B

1.
```
    □
  □    14
 3  8   □
```

2.
```
    □
 17   13
  □  9   □
```

3.
```
      28
   □    □
  □  7   9
```

4.
```
    □
 19    13
 13  □   □
```

5.
```
    37
 17    □
  □  11   □
```

6.
```
    29
  □    14
  □  □   7
```

C

1.
```
      □
    □    □
   □  □   □
  8  3  5  7
```

2.
```
        □
      □    □
   13   □    14
    □  9   6   □
```

3.
```
       □
     □    29
    □   18   □
   2  □   □   4
```

4.
```
        63
     □     □
   14   □    □
  □  5   12   □
```

5.
```
        54
     □     25
    □   12    □
  □  7   □    □
```

TARGET To recall and use ×/÷ facts for 2, 5 and 10.

A

Work out

1. 7×2
2. 10×2
3. 12×2
4. 8×2

5. 6×5
6. 9×5
7. 5×5
8. 10×5

9. 3×10
10. 6×10
11. 12×10
12. 9×10

13. $10 \div 2$
14. $22 \div 2$
15. $18 \div 2$
16. $12 \div 2$

17. $40 \div 5$
18. $20 \div 5$
19. $60 \div 5$
20. $35 \div 5$

21. $70 \div 10$
22. $100 \div 10$
23. $10 \div 10$
24. $50 \div 10$

B

Copy and complete.

1. $\square \times 2 = 8$
2. $\square \times 5 = 50$
3. $7 \times \square = 70$
4. $6 \times \square = 30$

5. $\square \times 2 = 20$
6. $\square \times 10 = 110$
7. $6 \times \square = 12$
8. $10 \times \square = 100$

9. $\square \times 10 = 60$
10. $\square \times 5 = 25$
11. $9 \times \square = 18$
12. $11 \times \square = 55$

13. $\square \div 2 = 7$
14. $\square \div 10 = 8$
15. $24 \div \square = 12$
16. $45 \div \square = 9$

17. $\square \div 10 = 5$
18. $\square \div 2 = 8$
19. $120 \div \square = 12$
20. $20 \div \square = 4$

21. $\square \div 10 = 9$
22. $\square \div 5 = 7$
23. $10 \div \square = 5$
24. $40 \div \square = 8$

C

Work out the brackets first. Write the answers only.

1. $(4 \times 2) + (7 \times 10)$
2. $(8 \times 5) + (8 \times 2)$
3. $(1 \times 10) + (12 \times 5)$
4. $(6 \times 10) + (5 \times 2)$

5. $(10 \times 2) + (11 \times 5)$
6. $(9 \times 5) + (4 \times 10)$
7. $(10 \times 10) - (3 \times 5)$
8. $(7 \times 5) - (6 \times 2)$

9. $(8 \times 10) - (9 \times 2)$
10. $(12 \times 10) - (10 \times 5)$
11. $(6 \times 5) - (11 \times 2)$
12. $(9 \times 10) - (7 \times 2)$

Copy and complete the multiplication squares.

13.

×	5	2	10
7			
12			
9			

14.

×			
2			22
10	50		
5		40	

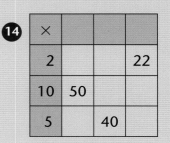

TARGET   To recall and use ×/÷ facts for 3.

A

Work out

1. 4×3
2. 10×3
3. 2×3
4. 8×3

5. 6×3
6. 1×3
7. 11×3
8. 3×3

9. 7×3
10. 12×3
11. 9×3
12. 5×3

13. $15 \div 3$
14. $24 \div 3$
15. $9 \div 3$
16. $30 \div 3$

17. $6 \div 3$
18. $33 \div 3$
19. $21 \div 3$
20. $12 \div 3$

21. $3 \div 3$
22. $27 \div 3$
23. $18 \div 3$
24. $36 \div 3$

B

Copy and complete.

1. $\square \times 3 = 21$
2. $\square \times 3 = 12$
3. $\square \div 3 = 10$
4. $\square \div 3 = 6$

5. $\square \times 3 = 36$
6. $\square \times 3 = 27$
7. $\square \div 3 = 8$
8. $\square \div 3 = 11$

9. $\square \times 3 = 9$
10. $\square \times 3 = 18$
11. $\square \div 3 = 12$
12. $\square \div 3 = 7$

13. $\square \times 3 = 30$
14. $\square \times 3 = 24$
15. $\square \div 3 = 4$
16. $\square \div 3 = 1$

17. $\square \times 3 = 33$
18. $\square \times 3 = 15$
19. $\square \div 3 = 3$
20. $\square \div 3 = 9$

21. There are three children in each group. How many children are there in:

    a) 6 groups
    b) 30 groups
    c) 12 groups?

C

Work out

1. 40×3
2. 90×3
3. 20×3
4. 70×3
5. 50×3
6. 80×3
7. 30×3
8. 60×3
9. $240 \div 3$
10. $150 \div 3$
11. $300 \div 3$
12. $180 \div 3$
13. $120 \div 3$
14. $60 \div 3$
15. $270 \div 3$
16. $210 \div 3$

Work out by multiplying by 3 and doubling.

17. 4×6
18. 7×6
19. 11×6
20. 9×6
21. 50×6
22. 80×6
23. 30×6
24. 60×6

Work out by halving and dividing by 3.

25. $18 \div 6$
26. $42 \div 6$
27. $30 \div 6$
28. $48 \div 6$
29. $36 \div 6$
30. $54 \div 6$
31. $24 \div 6$
32. $72 \div 6$

33. There are six apples in each pack. How many packs can be made from:

    a) 54 apples
    b) 240 apples
    c) 150 apples?

TARGET To recall and use ×/÷ facts for 4.

A
Work out

1. 3×4
2. 6×4
3. 1×4
4. 8×4

5. 10×4
6. 4×4
7. 11×4
8. 2×4

9. 9×4
10. 12×4
11. 5×4
12. 7×4

13. $40 \div 4$
14. $16 \div 4$
15. $24 \div 4$
16. $4 \div 4$

17. $32 \div 4$
18. $12 \div 4$
19. $48 \div 4$
20. $28 \div 4$

21. $8 \div 4$
22. $44 \div 4$
23. $20 \div 4$
24. $36 \div 4$

B
Copy and complete.

1. $\square \times 4 = 20$
2. $\square \times 4 = 32$
3. $\square \div 4 = 6$
4. $\square \div 4 = 12$

5. $\square \times 4 = 12$
6. $\square \times 4 = 40$
7. $\square \div 4 = 4$
8. $\square \div 4 = 8$

9. $\square \times 4 = 44$
10. $\square \times 4 = 24$
11. $\square \div 4 = 1$
12. $\square \div 4 = 9$

13. $\square \times 4 = 16$
14. $\square \times 4 = 28$
15. $\square \div 4 = 5$
16. $\square \div 4 = 10$

17. $\square \times 4 = 48$
18. $\square \times 4 = 36$
19. $\square \div 4 = 11$
20. $\square \div 4 = 7$

21. There are four walls in each room. How many walls are there in:
    a) 8 rooms
    b) 15 rooms
    c) 21 rooms?

C
Work out

1. 40×4
2. 90×4
3. 30×4
4. 60×4

5. 50×4
6. 70×4
7. 20×4
8. 80×4

9. $120 \div 4$
10. $240 \div 4$
11. $200 \div 4$
12. $280 \div 4$

13. $400 \div 4$
14. $320 \div 4$
15. $160 \div 4$
16. $360 \div 4$

Work out by multiplying by 4 and doubling.

17. 5×8
18. 7×8
19. 3×8
20. 6×8

21. 12×8
22. 9×8
23. 4×8
24. 8×8

Work out by halving and dividing by 4.

25. $24 \div 8$
26. $48 \div 8$
27. $16 \div 8$
28. $72 \div 8$

29. $40 \div 8$
30. $64 \div 8$
31. $88 \div 8$
32. $56 \div 8$

33. There are eight fish in each packet. How many packets can be made from:
    a) 32 fish
    b) 400 fish
    c) 104 fish?

TARGET To recall and use ×/÷ facts for 2, 3, 4, 5 and 10.

A

What is

1. 7×2
2. 4×5
3. 12×10
4. 10×2

5. $110 \div 10$
6. $25 \div 5$
7. $16 \div 2$
8. $40 \div 10$

9. 9×5
10. 5×2
11. 8×10
12. 7×5

13. $22 \div 2$
14. $100 \div 10$
15. $40 \div 5$
16. $18 \div 2$

17. 5×10
18. 12×2
19. 11×5
20. 9×10

21. $30 \div 5$
22. $12 \div 2$
23. $70 \div 10$
24. $60 \div 5$

B

Copy and complete.

1. $\square \times 5 = 10$
2. $\square \times 2 = 14$
3. $\square \div 10 = 7$
4. $\square \div 5 = 6$

5. $\square \times 10 = 90$
6. $\square \times 2 = 24$
7. $\square \div 5 = 10$
8. $\square \div 2 = 5$

9. $\square \times 5 = 55$
10. $\square \times 10 = 120$
11. $\square \div 2 = 8$
12. $\square \div 10 = 10$

Write the answer only.

13. 5×3
14. 8×3
15. 3×4
16. 10×4

17. 2×3
18. 7×3
19. 10×4
20. 9×4

21. 4×3
22. 11×3
23. 1×4
24. 6×4

25. $30 \div 3$
26. $24 \div 3$
27. $16 \div 4$
28. $44 \div 4$

29. $3 \div 3$
30. $18 \div 3$
31. $20 \div 4$
32. $28 \div 4$

33. $36 \div 3$
34. $27 \div 3$
35. $48 \div 4$
36. $32 \div 4$

C

Copy and complete.

1. $\square \times 3 = 21$
2. $\square \times 4 = 36$
3. $\square \div 3 = 5$
4. $\square \div 4 = 11$

5. $\square \times 3 = 3$
6. $\square \times 4 = 20$
7. $\square \div 3 = 12$
8. $\square \div 4 = 6$

9. $\square \times 3 = 27$
10. $\square \times 4 = 48$
11. $\square \div 3 = 10$
12. $\square \div 4 = 8$

Write the answer only.

13. 20×3
14. 100×4
15. 70×3
16. 90×4

17. 40×3
18. 120×4
19. 110×3
20. 80×4

21. 90×3
22. 40×4
23. 30×3
24. 70×4

25. $180 \div 3$
26. $120 \div 4$
27. $300 \div 3$
28. $440 \div 4$

29. $240 \div 3$
30. $360 \div 4$
31. $150 \div 3$
32. $240 \div 4$

33. $210 \div 3$
34. $80 \div 4$
35. $360 \div 3$
36. $320 \div 4$

TARGET To recall and use ×/÷ facts for 8.

A

Double and double again to multiply by 4.

1. 5
2. 11
3. 3
4. 7
5. 10
6. 4
7. 9
8. 6
9. 12
10. 8

Double, double and double again to multiply by 8.

11. 10
12. 6
13. 2
14. 12
15. 7
16. 5
17. 8
18. 11
19. 4
20. 9

21. Copy and complete by doubling.

TIMES TABLES		
Twos	Fours	Eights
2		
4		
6		
8		
10		
12		
14		
16		
18		
20		
22		
24		

B

Write the answers only.

1. 4 × 8
2. 6 × 8
3. 12 × 8
4. 9 × 8
5. 5 × 8
6. 10 × 8
7. 7 × 8
8. 3 × 8
9. 11 × 8
10. 8 × 8
11. 40 ÷ 8
12. 8 ÷ 8
13. 88 ÷ 8
14. 56 ÷ 8
15. 32 ÷ 8
16. 72 ÷ 8
17. 16 ÷ 8
18. 64 ÷ 8
19. 96 ÷ 8
20. 48 ÷ 8

Copy and complete.

21. ☐ × 8 = 56
22. ☐ × 8 = 16
23. ☐ × 8 = 72
24. ☐ × 8 = 96
25. ☐ × 8 = 48
26. ☐ × 8 = 24
27. ☐ × 8 = 80
28. ☐ × 8 = 64
29. ☐ ÷ 8 = 4
30. ☐ ÷ 8 = 7
31. ☐ ÷ 8 = 10
32. ☐ ÷ 8 = 6
33. ☐ ÷ 8 = 11
34. ☐ ÷ 8 = 8
35. ☐ ÷ 8 = 5
36. ☐ ÷ 8 = 9

C

Write the answers only.

1. 30 × 8
2. 90 × 8
3. 40 × 8
4. 80 × 8
5. 60 × 8
6. 20 × 8
7. 50 × 8
8. 70 × 8
9. 640 ÷ 8
10. 240 ÷ 8
11. 480 ÷ 8
12. 960 ÷ 8
13. 400 ÷ 8
14. 560 ÷ 8
15. 880 ÷ 8
16. 720 ÷ 8

Work out by multiplying by 8 and doubling.

17. 4 × 16
18. 7 × 16
19. 3 × 16
20. 6 × 16
21. 11 × 16
22. 9 × 16
23. 5 × 16
24. 10 × 16
25. 8 × 16
26. 12 × 16

27. Maurice earns £8 per hour. How much does he earn if he works 37 hours in a week?

28. There are eight cookies in each packet.

   a) How many cookies are needed to make 68 packets?

   b) How many packets can be made from 280 cookies?

29. What is 8 times 8 times 8?

TARGET To connect the 2, 4 and 8 times tables by doubling and halving.

Example 1 30 × 8
Double 30, double and double again to multiply by 8.
30 → 60 → 120 → 240
Answer *240*

Example 2 1000 ÷ 8
Halve 1000, halve and halve again to divide by 8.
1000 → 500 → 250 → 125
Answer *125*

A

Double and double again to multiply each number by 4.

❶ 3   ❺ 12

❷ 40   ❻ 25

❸ 15   ❼ 90

❹ 7   ❽ 21

Halve and halve again to divide each number by 4.

❾ 40   ⓭ 20

❿ 28   ⓮ 44

⓫ 120   ⓯ 24

⓬ 32   ⓰ 60

Use squared paper. Draw each shape half the size of the measurements shown.

⓱

10 cm
14 cm

⓲
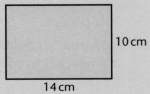
16 cm
4 cm
4 cm
8 cm
8 cm   8 cm

B

Double, double and double again to multiply each number by 8.

❶ 8   ❺ 6

❷ 13   ❻ 20

❸ 25   ❼ 55

❹ 70   ❽ 18

Halve, halve and halve again to divide each number by 8.

❾ 600   ⓭ 120

❿ 88   ⓮ 640

⓫ 40   ⓯ 360

⓬ 480   ⓰ 112

⓱ Use squared paper. Draw the flag half the size of the measurements shown.

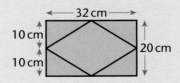
32 cm
10 cm
10 cm
20 cm

⓲ Now draw the flag one quarter the size of the measurements shown.

C

Copy and complete.

❶ ☐ × 8 = 4000

❷ ☐ × 8 = 248

❸ ☐ × 8 = 296

❹ ☐ × 8 = 280

❺ ☐ ÷ 8 = 60

❻ ☐ ÷ 8 = 23

❼ ☐ ÷ 8 = 95

❽ ☐ ÷ 8 = 17

Double the first answer to work out the second.

❾ 20 × 6   ⓫ 7 × 8
20 × 12   7 × 16

❿ 5 × 9   ⓬ 11 × 7
5 × 18   11 × 14

⓭ Use squared paper. Draw the flag one quarter the size of the measurements shown.

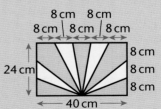
8 cm   8 cm
8 cm   8 cm   8 cm
8 cm
8 cm
24 cm
8 cm
40 cm

⓮ Now draw the flag one eighth size.

TARGET   To recall and use ×/÷ facts for 2, 3, 4, 5, 8 and 10.

A

What is

1. 8×2
2. 5×2
3. 12×2
4. 7×2

5. 6×5
6. 9×5
7. 7×5
8. 11×5

9. 3×10
10. 9×10
11. 6×10
12. 8×10

13. $12 \div 2$
14. $18 \div 2$
15. $6 \div 2$
16. $24 \div 2$

17. $50 \div 5$
18. $25 \div 5$
19. $60 \div 5$
20. $40 \div 5$

21. $40 \div 10$
22. $100 \div 10$
23. $70 \div 10$
24. $120 \div 10$

B

Copy and complete.

1. $\square \times 2 = 14$
2. $\square \times 5 = 20$
3. $\square \div 10 = 11$
4. $\square \div 2 = 9$

5. $\square \times 10 = 80$
6. $\square \times 2 = 12$
7. $\square \div 5 = 12$
8. $\square \div 10 = 5$

9. $\square \times 5 = 35$
10. $\square \times 10 = 60$
11. $\square \div 2 = 12$
12. $\square \div 5 = 9$

Write the answer only.

13. 6×3 25. $27 \div 3$
14. 3×4 26. $28 \div 4$
15. 11×8 27. $64 \div 8$
16. 8×3 28. $9 \div 3$

17. 12×4 29. $44 \div 4$
18. 6×8 30. $96 \div 8$
19. 11×3 31. $21 \div 3$
20. 7×4 32. $12 \div 4$

21. 9×8 33. $40 \div 8$
22. 5×3 34. $36 \div 3$
23. 8×4 35. $32 \div 4$
24. 7×8 36. $80 \div 8$

C

Copy and complete.

1. $\square \times 4 = 24$
2. $\square \times 8 = 56$
3. $\square \div 3 = 3$
4. $\square \div 4 = 9$

5. $\square \times 8 = 88$
6. $\square \times 3 = 30$
7. $\square \div 4 = 5$
8. $\square \div 8 = 6$

9. $\square \times 3 = 24$
10. $\square \times 4 = 48$
11. $\square \div 8 = 9$
12. $\square \div 3 = 1$

Write the answer only.

13. 70×4 25. $120 \div 4$
14. 100×8 26. $720 \div 8$
15. 90×3 27. $330 \div 3$
16. 120×4 28. $320 \div 4$

17. 50×8 29. $160 \div 8$
18. 60×3 30. $150 \div 3$
19. 90×4 31. $400 \div 4$
20. 30×8 32. $480 \div 8$

21. 40×3 33. $60 \div 3$
22. 110×4 34. $160 \div 4$
23. 80×8 35. $960 \div 8$
24. 120×3 36. $210 \div 3$

TARGET   To multiply multiples of 10 by one-digit numbers.

Examples

$90 \times 2 = 10 \times 9 \times 2$

$\qquad = 10 \times 18$

$\qquad = 180$

$8 \times 4 = 32$

$80 \times 4 = 320$

$3 \times 5 = 15$

$3 \times 50 = 150$

A

Multiply by 10.

1. 3
2. 8
3. 2
4. 6
5. 4
6. 7
7. 5
8. 9

Copy and complete.

9. $40 \times 2 = 10 \times 4 \times 2$
   $= 10 \times \square$
   $= \square$

10. $50 \times 4 = 10 \times \square \times 4$
    $= 10 \times \square$
    $= \square$

11. $80 \times 5 = 10 \times \square \times 5$
    $= 10 \times \square$
    $= \square$

12. $30 \times 3 = 10 \times \square \times \square$
    $= \square \times \square$
    $= \square$

13. $70 \times 2 = 10 \times 7 \times \square$
    $= 10 \times \square$
    $= \square$

14. $20 \times 5 = \square \times \square \times \square$
    $= \square \times \square$
    $= \square$

Work out

15. 80×4
16. 20×2
17. 50×3
18. 60×5
19. 90×2
20. 20×4
21. 30×5
22. 60×3

B

Copy and complete.

1. $3 \times 4 = \square$
   $30 \times 4 = \square$

2. $5 \times 5 = \square$
   $50 \times 5 = \square$

3. $3 \times 2 = \square$
   $30 \times 2 = \square$

4. $7 \times 3 = \square$
   $7 \times 30 = \square$

5. $2 \times 8 = \square$
   $2 \times 80 = \square$

6. $6 \times 4 = \square$
   $6 \times 40 = \square$

Write the answer only.

7. 40×5
8. 20×3
9. 80×8
10. 50×2
11. 40×3
12. 80×2
13. 90×5
14. 70×4
15. 9×40
16. 7×50
17. 8×30
18. 4×80

C

Copy and complete.

1. $60 \times \square = 300$
2. $\square \times 4 = 280$
3. $8 \times \square = 160$
4. $\square \times 70 = 140$
5. $\square \times 8 = 240$
6. $30 \times \square = 180$
7. $\square \times 90 = 360$
8. $7 \times \square = 210$

Work out

9. 900×3
10. 500×6
11. 800×5
12. 900×8
13. 500×7
14. 9×400
15. 6×200
16. 3×900
17. 4×700
18. 6×800

Work out

19. 70×50
20. 30×70
21. 90×20
22. 50×90
23. 20×60
24. 80×40
25. 20×90
26. 60×30
27. 80×80
28. 40×60

TARGET To multiply multiples of 10 by one-digit numbers.

Examples

$8 \times 4 = 32$
$8 \times 40 = 320$

$5 \times 3 = 15$
$50 \times 3 = 150$

How much is six 20p coins?

$20p \times 6 = 120p$
$= £1·20$

A

Copy and complete.

1. $2 \times 3 = \boxed{}$
   $20 \times 3 = \boxed{}$
2. $5 \times 5 = \boxed{}$
   $50 \times 5 = \boxed{}$
3. $4 \times 2 = \boxed{}$
   $4 \times 20 = \boxed{}$
4. $3 \times 8 = \boxed{}$
   $3 \times 80 = \boxed{}$
5. $8 \times 4 = \boxed{}$
   $80 \times 4 = \boxed{}$
6. $3 \times 5 = \boxed{}$
   $30 \times 5 = \boxed{}$
7. $9 \times 3 = \boxed{}$
   $9 \times 30 = \boxed{}$
8. $2 \times 8 = \boxed{}$
   $2 \times 80 = \boxed{}$

Work out

9. 5×20
10. 4×40
11. 60×5
12. 40×8
13. 7×30
14. 6×20
15. 20×4
16. 90×5

17. How much is eight 20p coins?
18. How much is three 50p coins?

B

Write the answer only.

1. 5×30
2. 6×40
3. 20×2
4. 80×5
5. 6×80
6. 9×40
7. 70×2
8. 30×3
9. 4×50
10. 9×80
11. 80×3
12. 90×2
13. 2×50
14. 8×80
15. 30×4
16. 60×3

17. What is the total weight of seven 50 g weights?

18. Bennie takes four 20 ml doses of medicine every day. How much medicine does he take
    a) in a day
    b) in a week?

19. How much is forty £5 notes?

20. Ice creams are 90p each. How much do four ice creams cost?

C

Copy and complete.

1. $50 \times \boxed{} = 400$
2. $\boxed{} \times 5 = 450$
3. $8 \times \boxed{} = 160$
4. $\boxed{} \times 60 = 180$
5. $70 \times \boxed{} = 280$
6. $\boxed{} \times 9 = 180$
7. $9 \times \boxed{} = 270$
8. $\boxed{} \times 70 = 210$

Write the answer only.

9. 8×300
10. 4×600
11. 6×200
12. 5×500
13. 3×900
14. 200×7
15. 400×4
16. 900×8
17. 700×3
18. 600×5

Work out

19. 70×50
20. 80×40
21. 40×70
22. 90×20
23. 50×60
24. 15×30
25. 17×20
26. 24×50
27. 32×40
28. 28×30

TARGET   To multiply multiples of 10 by single-digit numbers.

Examples

$6 \times 4 = 24$ $5 \times 7 = 35$ What is the total $50\,g \times 3 = 150\,g$

$6 \times 40 = 240$ $5 \times 70 = 350$ weight of three

                                         50 g weights?

A

Work out

1. 20×5 9. 4×20
2. 20×2 10. 8×50
3. 30×8 11. 3×30
4. 50×3 12. 4×40
5. 20×4 13. 7×20
6. 60×5 14. 2×30
7. 90×2 15. 5×50
8. 50×8 16. 2×80

17. Laura has four 50p coins. How much does she have altogether?

18. There are 20 books in each pile. There are eight piles. How many books are there altogether?

19. Each pack has 40 nappies. How many nappies are there in three packs?

20. There are 30 trees in each row and four rows in the orchard. How many trees are there in the orchard?

B

Work out

1. 30×2 9. 2×90
2. 40×8 10. 3×40
3. 60×3 11. 7×80
4. 70×4 12. 9×30
5. 30×6 13. 6×20
6. 50×2 14. 4×60
7. 40×5 15. 9×80
8. 80×3 16. 8×40

17. One stamp costs 90p. What do three stamps cost?

18. Each bag holds 50 coins. How many coins are there in eight bags?

19. Tubes of toothpaste weigh 80 g. What is the total weight of the toothpaste in six tubes?

20. A car travels at a steady speed of 70 miles per hour for three hours. How far has the car travelled?

C

Work out

1. 200×6 9. 60×40
2. 700×3 10. 70×90
3. 900×8 11. 40×70
4. 600×9 12. 80×60
5. 8×700 13. 600×3
6. 3×600 14. 800×8
7. 8×200 15. 700×5
8. 7×800 16. 500×9

17. There are 200 raffle tickets in each book. Seven books of tickets are sold. How many tickets are sold altogether?

18. Each can of beans weighs 400 g. What is the total weight of nine cans?

19. Mina runs round the park four times. The distance round the park is 900 m. How far has Mina run altogether?

TARGET To divide 2-digit and 3-digit multiples of 10 by one-digit numbers.

Examples

$80 \div 4 = 10 \times 8 \div 4$
$\qquad = 10 \times 2$
$\qquad = 20$

$270 \div 3 = 10 \times 27 \div 3$
$\qquad = 10 \times 9$
$\qquad = 90$

A

Divide by 10.

1. 40
2. 70
3. 80
4. 50
5. 20
6. 90
7. 30
8. 60

Copy and complete.

9. $80 \div 2 = 10 \times 8 \div 2$
$\qquad = 10 \times \boxed{}$
$\qquad = \boxed{}$

10. $60 \div 3 = 10 \times \boxed{} \div 3$
$\qquad = 10 \times \boxed{}$
$\qquad = \boxed{}$

11. $450 \div 5 = 10 \times 45 \div \boxed{}$
$\qquad = \boxed{} \times \boxed{}$
$\qquad = \boxed{}$

12. $120 \div 4 = \boxed{} \times \boxed{} \div 4$
$\qquad = \boxed{} \times \boxed{}$
$\qquad = \boxed{}$

Work out

13. $200 \div 4$
14. $60 \div 2$
15. $100 \div 5$
16. $180 \div 3$
17. $160 \div 2$
18. $120 \div 4$
19. $240 \div 3$
20. $350 \div 7$

B

Copy and complete.

1. $12 \div 3 = \boxed{}$
$120 \div 3 = \boxed{}$

2. $8 \div 4 = \boxed{}$
$80 \div 4 = \boxed{}$

3. $10 \div 2 = \boxed{}$
$100 \div 2 = \boxed{}$

4. $15 \div 5 = \boxed{}$
$150 \div 5 = \boxed{}$

5. $40 \div 8 = \boxed{}$
$400 \div 8 = \boxed{}$

6. $21 \div 3 = \boxed{}$
$210 \div 3 = \boxed{}$

Write the answer only.

7. $240 \div 4$
8. $40 \div 2$
9. $320 \div 8$
10. $240 \div 3$
11. $120 \div 2$
12. $360 \div 4$
13. $400 \div 5$
14. $90 \div 3$
15. $250 \div 5$
16. $280 \div 4$
17. $180 \div 2$
18. $160 \div 8$

C

Copy and complete.

1. $560 \div \boxed{} = 80$
2. $\boxed{} \div 3 = 60$
3. $450 \div \boxed{} = 50$
4. $\boxed{} \div 7 = 20$
5. $160 \div \boxed{} = 80$
6. $\boxed{} \div 6 = 30$
7. $280 \div \boxed{} = 70$
8. $\boxed{} \div 9 = 40$

Work out

9. $1400 \div 2$
10. $3500 \div 7$
11. $3000 \div 5$
12. $2700 \div 9$
13. $3200 \div 4$
14. $1500 \div 3$
15. $4800 \div 8$
16. $2400 \div 6$

Work out

17. $120 \div 4$
18. $120 \div 40$
19. $2500 \div 5$
20. $2500 \div 50$
21. $180 \div 2$
22. $180 \div 20$
23. $7200 \div 8$
24. $7200 \div 80$
25. $1200 \div 20$
26. $1200 \div 200$
27. $4800 \div 6$
28. $4800 \div 60$

TARGET To divide 2-digit and 3-digit multiples of 10 by one-digit numbers.

Examples

$25 \div 5 = 5$ $16 \div 8 = 2$

$250 \div 5 = 50$ $160 \div 8 = 20$

A

Copy and complete.

1. $15 \div 5 = \square$

    $150 \div 5 = \square$

2. $12 \div 3 = \square$

    $120 \div 3 = \square$

3. $4 \div 2 = \square$

    $40 \div 2 = \square$

4. $36 \div 4 = \square$

    $360 \div 4 = \square$

5. $40 \div 8 = \square$

    $400 \div 8 = \square$

6. $21 \div 3 = \square$

    $210 \div 3 = \square$

7. $40 \div 5 = \square$

    $400 \div 5 = \square$

8. $18 \div 2 = \square$

    $180 \div 2 = \square$

Work out

9. $90 \div 3$

10. $320 \div 8$

11. $120 \div 2$

12. $80 \div 4$

13. $300 \div 5$

14. $240 \div 8$

15. $160 \div 4$

16. $240 \div 3$

B

Write the answer only.

1. $240 \div 4$ 9. $160 \div 2$

2. $200 \div 5$ 10. $720 \div 8$

3. $560 \div 8$ 11. $200 \div 4$

4. $60 \div 3$ 12. $100 \div 5$

5. $80 \div 2$ 13. $270 \div 3$

6. $350 \div 5$ 14. $480 \div 8$

7. $120 \div 4$ 15. $140 \div 2$

8. $180 \div 3$ 16. $320 \div 4$

17. How many bags of three can be made from 150 oranges?

18. There are 360 children in a school. The four year groups each have the same number of pupils. How many children are there in each year group?

19. A pie weighs 640 g. It is cut into eight equal slices. How much does each slice weigh?

20. How many 5p coins make £4·50?

C

Copy and complete.

1. $\square \div 2 = 90$

2. $280 \div \square = 70$

3. $\square \div 7 = 30$

4. $240 \div \square = 40$

5. $\square \div 5 = 60$

6. $450 \div \square = 50$

7. $\square \div 3 = 70$

8. $240 \div \square = 30$

Write the answer only.

9. $2100 \div 3$ 13. $1400 \div 2$

10. $3600 \div 4$ 14. $4800 \div 8$

11. $3200 \div 8$ 15. $4500 \div 5$

12. $4000 \div 5$ 16. $2400 \div 3$

Copy and complete.

17. $120 \div 4 = \square$

    $8 \div 4 = \square$

    $128 \div 4 = \square$

18. $180 \div 3 = \square$

    $15 \div 3 = \square$

    $195 \div 3 = \square$

Work out

19. $205 \div 5$ 23. $92 \div 4$

20. $126 \div 2$ 24. $258 \div 3$

21. $162 \div 3$ 25. $190 \div 2$

22. $96 \div 8$ 26. $375 \div 5$

TARGET To divide 3-digit multiples of 10 by one-digit numbers.

Examples

720 ÷ 8

72 ÷ 8 = 9
720 ÷ 8 = 90
Answer *90*

How many 5p coins make £2?

£2 = 200p
200 ÷ 5 = 40
Answer *40 coins*

A

Work out

1. 120 ÷ 3
2. 100 ÷ 2
3. 160 ÷ 8
4. 300 ÷ 5
5. 200 ÷ 4
6. 140 ÷ 2
7. 150 ÷ 3
8. 200 ÷ 5
9. 180 ÷ 2
10. 400 ÷ 8
11. 350 ÷ 5
12. 80 ÷ 4
13. 60 ÷ 2
14. 240 ÷ 3
15. 450 ÷ 5
16. 320 ÷ 8

17. Hannah sorts 120 books into four equal piles. How many books are there in each pile?

B

Work out

1. 80 ÷ 2
2. 210 ÷ 3
3. 240 ÷ 8
4. 100 ÷ 5
5. 240 ÷ 4
6. 300 ÷ 6
7. 90 ÷ 3
8. 640 ÷ 8
9. 280 ÷ 4
10. 450 ÷ 9
11. 160 ÷ 2
12. 180 ÷ 3
13. 480 ÷ 8
14. 400 ÷ 5
15. 140 ÷ 7
16. 360 ÷ 4

17. A minibus travels the same route every day. In five days it travels 250 miles. How long is the route?

18. Four chocolate eggs weigh 160 g. What does one egg weigh?

19. There are 9 biscuits in each pack. How many packs can be made from 180 biscuits?

20. Eight plane tickets cost £720. What does one ticket cost?

C

Work out

1. 1200 ÷ 6
2. 2700 ÷ 3
3. 3600 ÷ 9
4. 3500 ÷ 7
5. 2400 ÷ 6
6. 1800 ÷ 2
7. 3500 ÷ 5
8. 2700 ÷ 9
9. 280 ÷ 70
10. 320 ÷ 40
11. 180 ÷ 60
12. 560 ÷ 80
13. 7200 ÷ 90
14. 3000 ÷ 50
15. 4800 ÷ 60
16. 2100 ÷ 70

17. Each box holds four cakes. How many boxes are needed for 240 cakes?

18. How many 2 litre bottles of milk can be filled from 140 litres?

19. In seven days Kenya earns £560. How much does she earn daily?

20. Nine identical weights are put on a scale. Their combined weight is 450 g. What is each weight?

TARGET To develop a written method to multiply TU by U.

Examples

```
      3 6
  ×     4
  ─────────
      2 4    6 × 4
    1 2 0    30 × 4
  ─────────
    1 4 4
```

```
      3 6
  ×     4
  ─────────
    1 4 4
      2
```

6 × 4 = 24
20 is carried into tens (2)
4 is written in units (4)
30 × 4 = 120
120 + 24 = 144
Answer *144*

A

Copy and complete.

1
```
      2 6
  ×     2
```
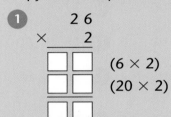
(6 × 2)
(20 × 2)

2
```
      5 9
  ×     5
```
(9 × 5)
(50 × 5)

3
```
      4 5
  ×     3
```

4
```
      2 4
  ×     4
```

Work out

5 68 × 2   **7** 57 × 3

6 36 × 5   **8** 35 × 4

B

Copy and complete.

1
```
    3 7
  ×   2
```
9
```
    2 5
  ×   5
```

2
```
    2 4
  ×   3
```
10
```
    9 7
  ×   4
```

3
```
    8 3
  ×   5
```
11
```
    8 5
  ×   2
```

4
```
    6 6
  ×   4
```
12
```
    6 9
  ×   3
```

5
```
    5 9
  ×   2
```
13
```
    5 5
  ×   4
```

6
```
    4 7
  ×   5
```
14
```
    9 3
  ×   2
```

7
```
    3 8
  ×   4
```
15
```
    3 6
  ×   3
```

8
```
    9 6
  ×   3
```
16
```
    6 4
  ×   5
```

17 Double 76.

18 How many is 48 fours?

C

Work out

1 75 × 5   **9** 182 × 4

2 86 × 3   **10** 175 × 2

3 48 × 2   **11** 168 × 5

4 93 × 4   **12** 247 × 3

5 78 × 3   **13** 356 × 2

6 87 × 2   **14** 287 × 5

7 69 × 4   **15** 169 × 3

8 96 × 5   **16** 274 × 4

17 There are eight sausages in each packet. How many sausages are there in 34 packets?

18 The smallest snake was 42 cm long. The largest was six times longer. How long was the largest snake?

19 The 283 visitors to a museum each pay £5 to enter. How much is taken in ticket sales altogether?

20 One glass holds 165 ml of drink. How much will four identical glasses hold?

TARGET   To use a written method to multiply TU by U.

Example

```
        7 3                7 3          3 × 5 = 15
    ×     5            ×     5          10 is carried into tens
    ─────────          ─────────        5 is written in units
        1 5   3 × 5        3 6 5        70 × 5 = 350
      3 5 0   70 × 5        1           350 + 10 = 360
    ─────────                           Answer 365
      3 6 5
```

A

Copy and complete.

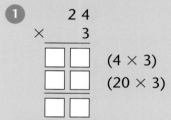

1
```
        2 4
    ×     3
```
    (4 × 3)
    (20 × 3)

2
```
        7 8
    ×     2
```
    (8 × 2)
    (70 × 2)

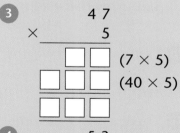

3
```
        4 7
    ×     5
```
    (7 × 5)
    (40 × 5)

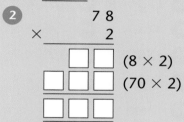

4
```
        5 3
    ×     4
```
    (3 × 4)
    (50 × 4)

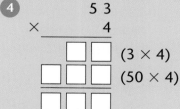

Work out

5 75 × 8   **9** 25 × 4

6 56 × 2   **10** 54 × 8

7 78 × 5   **11** 32 × 3

8 45 × 3   **12** 93 × 5

B

Copy and complete.

1
```
      64
    ×  4
```
  9
```
      65
    ×  2
```

2
```
      56
    ×  5
```
  10
```
      33
    ×  8
```

3
```
      37
    ×  3
```
  11
```
      87
    ×  4
```

4
```
      89
    ×  2
```
  12
```
      49
    ×  5
```

5
```
      46
    ×  8
```
  13
```
      76
    ×  3
```

6
```
      64
    ×  5
```
  14
```
      97
    ×  2
```

7
```
      98
    ×  4
```
  15
```
      89
    ×  8
```

8
```
      59
    ×  3
```
  16
```
      36
    ×  4
```

17 One pencil costs 28p. What do three cost?

18 What number is eight times larger than 75?

C

Work out

1 83 × 3   **9** 167 × 4

2 27 × 8   **10** 142 × 7

3 72 × 5   **11** 238 × 8

4 95 × 4   **12** 156 × 3

5 34 × 6   **13** 490 × 5

6 72 × 8   **14** 125 × 9

7 68 × 3   **15** 349 × 4

8 55 × 5   **16** 263 × 8

17 A school has six classes, each of which has 28 children. How many children are there in the school?

18 A castle is visited by 168 people on Wednesday and five times as many on Sunday. How many people visit the castle on Sunday?

TARGET To use a written method to multiply TU by U.

Examples

$$\begin{array}{r} 6\ 7 \\ \times\ \ \ 3 \\ \hline 2\ 1 \\ 1\ 8\ 0 \\ \hline 2\ 0\ 1 \end{array}$$

7×3
60×3

$$\begin{array}{r} 6\ 7 \\ \times\ \ \ 3 \\ \hline 2\ 0\ 1 \\ {\scriptstyle 2} \end{array}$$

$7 \times 3 = 21$
20 is carried into tens,
1 in units
$60 \times 3 = 180$
$180 + 20 = 200$
Answer *201*

A

Copy and complete.

1
$$\begin{array}{r} 3\ 9 \\ \times\ \ \ 5 \end{array}$$
□ □ (9 × 5)
□ □ □ (30 × 5)
□ □ □

2
$$\begin{array}{r} 6\ 5 \\ \times\ \ \ 2 \end{array}$$
□ □ (5 × 2)
□ □ □ (60 × 2)
□ □ □

3
$$\begin{array}{r} 3\ 7 \\ \times\ \ \ 4 \end{array}$$
□ □ (7 × 4)
□ □ □ (30 × 4)
□ □ □

4
$$\begin{array}{r} 2\ 3 \\ \times\ \ \ 8 \end{array}$$
□ □ (3 × 8)
□ □ □ (20 × 8)
□ □ □

Work out

5 56 × 3   **9** 35 × 8
6 67 × 5   **10** 82 × 5
7 24 × 4   **11** 29 × 3
8 88 × 2   **12** 48 × 4

B

Copy and complete.

1
$$\begin{array}{r} 3\ 5 \\ \times\ \ \ 3 \end{array}$$
9
$$\begin{array}{r} 4\ 6 \\ \times\ \ \ 8 \end{array}$$

2
$$\begin{array}{r} 7\ 8 \\ \times\ \ \ 5 \end{array}$$
10
$$\begin{array}{r} 7\ 9 \\ \times\ \ \ 4 \end{array}$$

3
$$\begin{array}{r} 9\ 4 \\ \times\ \ \ 2 \end{array}$$
11
$$\begin{array}{r} 6\ 5 \\ \times\ \ \ 5 \end{array}$$

4
$$\begin{array}{r} 5\ 2 \\ \times\ \ \ 8 \end{array}$$
12
$$\begin{array}{r} 4\ 8 \\ \times\ \ \ 3 \end{array}$$

5
$$\begin{array}{r} 6\ 5 \\ \times\ \ \ 4 \end{array}$$
13
$$\begin{array}{r} 7\ 6 \\ \times\ \ \ 2 \end{array}$$

6
$$\begin{array}{r} 9\ 3 \\ \times\ \ \ 5 \end{array}$$
14
$$\begin{array}{r} 6\ 9 \\ \times\ \ \ 8 \end{array}$$

7
$$\begin{array}{r} 8\ 7 \\ \times\ \ \ 3 \end{array}$$
15
$$\begin{array}{r} 5\ 7 \\ \times\ \ \ 4 \end{array}$$

8
$$\begin{array}{r} 5\ 6 \\ \times\ \ \ 2 \end{array}$$
16
$$\begin{array}{r} 9\ 4 \\ \times\ \ \ 3 \end{array}$$

17 How much is twenty four 5p's?

18 What is four times as many as 83?

C

Work out

1 358 × 2   **9** 709 × 5
2 569 × 3   **10** 386 × 4
3 284 × 5   **11** 514 × 9
4 437 × 8   **12** 895 × 3
5 153 × 4   **13** 328 × 8
6 325 × 6   **14** 196 × 5
7 286 × 3   **15** 250 × 7
8 174 × 8   **16** 478 × 3

17 There are 6 eggs in each box. How many eggs are there in 174 boxes?

18 One can of fish weighs 125 g. What do 8 cans weigh altogether?

19 There are 297 children in a Primary School. A nearby Secondary School has four times as many pupils. How many children go to the Secondary School?

20 The perimeter of a football pitch is 236 m. Dougie runs round the pitch nine times. How far does he run altogether?

TARGET To solve ×/÷ problems involving groups of numbers or quantities.

A

1. How many groups of 2 make four groups of 5?

2. How many groups of 3 make six groups of 2?

3. How many groups of 5 make ten groups of 3?

4. How many groups of 10 make five groups of 4?

Count up in groups.

5.

6.

7.

Use 30 counters.

8. How many groups of 10?

9. How many groups of 5?

10. How many groups of 3?

11. How many groups of 6?

12. How many groups of 10 make 50?

13. How many groups of 5 make 45?

14. How many groups of 2 make 14?

B

1. How many groups of 4 make eight groups of 3?

2. How many groups of 6 make three groups of 10?

3. How many groups of 2 make three groups of 8?

4. How many groups of 5 make two groups of 20?

How much money?

5. nine 10ps

6. seven 2ps

7. eight 5ps

8. three 20ps

Use 27 counters.

9. How many groups of 5?

10. How many groups of 3?

11. How many groups of 10?

12. How many groups of 4?

Fill in the box to make 100.

13. ☐ groups of 10?

14. ☐ groups of 20?

15. ☐ groups of 5?

16. ☐ groups of 50?

C

How much altogether?

1. seven 5ps, ten 2ps

2. one 50p, nine 2ps

3. three 20ps, five 5ps

4. four 20ps, six 2ps

Fill in the box to make £1.

5. ☐ 20ps   7. ☐ 50ps

6. ☐ 5ps   8. ☐ 2ps

9. There are five flowers in one bunch. How many flowers are there in 14 bunches?

10. There are 25 socks. How many pairs can be made? How many socks are left over?

11. How many biscuits are there in six packets if there are twenty biscuits in each packet?

12. How many weeks are there in 30 days? How many days are left over?

13. How many triangles can be made from 36 straws?

14. How many squares can be made from 27 straws. How many straws are left over?

TARGET   To develop a written method to divide TU by U.

Examples

72 ÷ 4
Repeated subtraction
(Chunking)

```
   7 2
-  4 0   (10 × 4)
  ----
   3 2
-  3 2   (8 × 4)
  ----
     0
```
Answer *18*

72 ÷ 4
Short division

```
    1 8
4)7³2
```

Step 1.   7 ÷ 4 = 1 remainder 3
Step 2.   32 ÷ 4 = 8

Answer *18*

A

Copy and complete.

1   85 ÷ 5

```
        8 5
-  □ □      (10 × 5)
   □ □
-  □ □      (□ × 5)
     0
```
Answer = □ □

2   46 ÷ 2

```
        4 6
-  □ □      (20 × 2)
   □ □
-  □ □      (□ × 2)
     0
```
Answer = □ □

Work out

3 32 ÷ 2   **9** 45 ÷ 3

4 55 ÷ 5   **10** 56 ÷ 4

5 48 ÷ 4   **11** 54 ÷ 2

6 33 ÷ 3   **12** 39 ÷ 3

7 70 ÷ 5   **13** 60 ÷ 5

8 78 ÷ 2   **14** 64 ÷ 4

B

Work out

1 64 ÷ 2   **9** 90 ÷ 5

2 75 ÷ 5   **10** 60 ÷ 4

3 51 ÷ 3   **11** 52 ÷ 2

4 90 ÷ 2   **12** 84 ÷ 3

5 92 ÷ 4   **13** 96 ÷ 2

6 65 ÷ 5   **14** 68 ÷ 4

7 58 ÷ 2   **15** 96 ÷ 3

8 99 ÷ 3   **16** 72 ÷ 2

17 Three friends equally share 42 sweets. How many do they have each?

18 Four children sit at each table. How many tables are needed for 52 children?

19 Seventy-four apples are shared equally between two barrels. How many apples are there in each barrel?

20 How many £5 notes make £95?

C

Work out

1 129 ÷ 3   **9** 135 ÷ 5

2 170 ÷ 5   **10** 116 ÷ 2

3 108 ÷ 4   **11** 108 ÷ 9

4 144 ÷ 2   **12** 184 ÷ 4

5 120 ÷ 8   **13** 117 ÷ 3

6 178 ÷ 2   **14** 130 ÷ 2

7 128 ÷ 4   **15** 84 ÷ 6

8 91 ÷ 7   **16** 104 ÷ 8

17 Ricky is half way through his book. It has 152 pages. How many pages has he read?

18 Each tray holds eight plants. How many trays are needed for 174 plants?

19 125 coins are shared equally between five bags. How many coins are there in each bag?

TARGET To use a written method to divide TU by U.

Examples

$68 \div 4$
(Chunking)

$$
\begin{array}{r}
6\,8 \\
-\,4\,0 \\ \hline
2\,8 \\
-\,2\,8 \\ \hline
0
\end{array}
$$

(10×4)

(7×4)

Answer *17*

$68 \div 4$
Short division

$$
\begin{array}{r}
1\,7 \\
4\overline{)6^{2}8}
\end{array}
$$

Step 1 $6 \div 4 = 1$ remainder 2

$28 \div 4 = 7$

Answer *17*

A

Copy and complete.

1 $95 \div 5$

$$
\begin{array}{r}
9\;\;5 \\
-\;\square\square \\ \hline
\square\square \\
-\;\square\square \\ \hline
0
\end{array}
$$

(10×5)

$(\square \times 5)$

Answer $= \square\square$

2 $70 \div 2$

$$
\begin{array}{r}
7\;\;0 \\
-\;\square\square \\ \hline
\square\square \\
-\;\square\square \\ \hline
0
\end{array}
$$

(30×2)

$(\square \times 2)$

Answer $= \square\square$

Work out

3 $60 \div 5$ **9** $80 \div 5$

4 $42 \div 3$ **10** $62 \div 2$

5 $52 \div 4$ **11** $51 \div 3$

6 $34 \div 2$ **12** $72 \div 4$

7 $66 \div 3$ **13** $75 \div 5$

8 $60 \div 4$ **14** $58 \div 2$

B

Work out

1 $32 \div 2$ **9** $94 \div 2$

2 $69 \div 3$ **10** $56 \div 4$

3 $65 \div 5$ **11** $88 \div 8$

4 $76 \div 4$ **12** $78 \div 3$

5 $68 \div 2$ **13** $90 \div 5$

6 $70 \div 5$ **14** $78 \div 2$

7 $45 \div 3$ **15** $84 \div 4$

8 $36 \div 2$ **16** $54 \div 3$

17 Elaine has been in her new job for 85 working days. She works 5 days each week. How many weeks has she worked?

18 A bike costs £90. How much will it cost in a half price sale?

19 Cards are sold in boxes of 4. How many boxes are needed for 64 cards?

20 Three lollies cost 87p altogether. How much does one lolly cost?

C

Work out

1 $148 \div 2$ **9** $190 \div 5$

2 $84 \div 7$ **10** $207 \div 3$

3 $125 \div 5$ **11** $105 \div 7$

4 $78 \div 6$ **12** $194 \div 2$

5 $111 \div 3$ **13** $116 \div 4$

6 $126 \div 9$ **14** $112 \div 8$

7 $180 \div 4$ **15** $144 \div 3$

8 $128 \div 8$ **16** $72 \div 6$

17 One dose of medicine is 10 ml. A bottle holds 200 ml. How many doses does it hold?

18 Eight people can sit on one row of chairs. How many rows are needed for 104 people?

19 A party of 162 children is divided equally between three coaches. How many children are in each coach?

20 Potatoes are sold in packs of 4. How many packs can be made from 148 potatoes?

TARGET　To use a written method to divide TU by U.

Examples　$75 \div 3$
(Chunking)

$$
\begin{array}{rl}
7\,5 & \\
-\,6\,0 & (20 \times 3) \\
\hline
1\,5 & \\
-\,1\,5 & (5 \times 3) \\
\hline
0 &
\end{array}
$$

Answer *25*

$75 \div 3$
Short division

$$
\begin{array}{r}
2\,5 \\
3\overline{)7\,^15}
\end{array}
$$

Step 1　$7 \div 3 = 2$ remainder 1
Step 2　$15 \div 3 = 5$

Answer *25*

A

Copy and complete.

1　$75 \div 5$

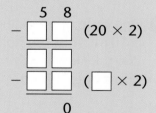

$$
\begin{array}{rl}
7\quad5 & \\
-\,\square\square & (10 \times 5) \\
\square\square & \\
-\,\square\square & (\square \times 5) \\
\hline
0 &
\end{array}
$$

Answer = □□

2　$58 \div 2$

$$
\begin{array}{rl}
5\quad8 & \\
-\,\square\square & (20 \times 2) \\
\square\square & \\
-\,\square\square & (\square \times 2) \\
\hline
0 &
\end{array}
$$

Answer = □□

Work out

3　$56 \div 4$　　**9**　$54 \div 3$

4　$84 \div 2$　　**10**　$65 \div 5$

5　$90 \div 5$　　**11**　$60 \div 2$

6　$69 \div 3$　　**12**　$64 \div 4$

7　$48 \div 2$　　**13**　$45 \div 3$

8　$92 \div 4$　　**14**　$70 \div 5$

B

Copy and complete.

1　$3\overline{)57}$　　**9**　$2\overline{)86}$

2　$5\overline{)80}$　　**10**　$4\overline{)96}$

3　$2\overline{)82}$　　**11**　$3\overline{)72}$

4　$4\overline{)88}$　　**12**　$2\overline{)54}$

5　$5\overline{)95}$　　**13**　$5\overline{)85}$

6　$2\overline{)76}$　　**14**　$8\overline{)96}$

7　$3\overline{)93}$　　**15**　$2\overline{)98}$

8　$4\overline{)72}$　　**16**　$3\overline{)48}$

17　Fifty-two paint brushes are divided equally between four pots. How many brushes are in each pot?

18　Cleo saves 2p coins. She has saved 74p altogether. How many coins has she saved?

19　The 81 children in Year 3 are split into three equal classes. How many children are in each class?

20　How many 5 cm lengths can be cut from 90 cm of string?

C

Copy and complete.

1　$4\overline{)172}$　　**9**　$2\overline{)112}$

2　$8\overline{)120}$　　**10**　$6\overline{)108}$

3　$2\overline{)126}$　　**11**　$5\overline{)145}$

4　$5\overline{)230}$　　**12**　$8\overline{)152}$

5　$6\overline{)66}$　　**13**　$7\overline{)98}$

6　$3\overline{)171}$　　**14**　$6\overline{)90}$

7　$9\overline{)135}$　　**15**　$3\overline{)228}$

8　$4\overline{)216}$　　**16**　$9\overline{)117}$

17　Five cakes cost £1·75 altogether. What does one cake cost?

18　Footballs cost £8 each. A school pays £136 for its new balls. How many have been bought?

19　Three friends share a bingo prize of £204. How much do they each get?

TARGET To use a written method to multiply or divide TU by U.

Examples

$$\begin{array}{r} 9\,4 \\ \times \quad 5 \\ \hline 2\,0 \\ 4\,5\,0 \\ \hline 4\,7\,0 \end{array}$$ (4 × 5)
(90 × 5)

or $$\begin{array}{r} 9\,4 \\ \times \quad 5 \\ \hline 4\,7\,0 \\ {\scriptstyle 2} \end{array}$$

72 ÷ 4

$$\begin{array}{r} 7\,2 \\ -\,4\,0 \\ \hline 3\,2 \\ -\,3\,2 \\ \hline 0 \end{array}$$ (10 × 4)
(8 × 4)

Answer *18*

or $4\overline{)7^3 2}$ with 1 8 above

Answer *18*

A

Copy and complete.

1
$$\begin{array}{r} 2\,6 \\ \times \quad 4 \end{array}$$

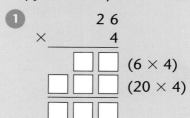

(6 × 4)
(20 × 4)

2 78 ÷ 3

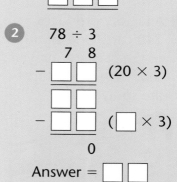

7 8
− ☐☐ (20 × 3)
− ☐☐ (☐ × 3)
0

Answer = ☐☐

Work out, using the method above.

3 54 × 3   **11** 70 ÷ 5

4 75 × 2   **12** 90 ÷ 2

5 43 × 5   **13** 68 ÷ 4

6 22 × 8   **14** 88 ÷ 8

7 19 × 3   **15** 51 ÷ 3

8 35 × 4   **16** 78 ÷ 2

9 39 × 2   **17** 65 ÷ 5

10 15 × 8   **18** 60 ÷ 4

B

Copy and complete.

1 $\begin{array}{r}59\\ \times\ 2\end{array}$ **5** $\begin{array}{r}85\\ \times\ 3\end{array}$

2 $\begin{array}{r}48\\ \times\ 4\end{array}$ **6** $\begin{array}{r}59\\ \times\ 4\end{array}$

3 $\begin{array}{r}65\\ \times\ 5\end{array}$ **7** $\begin{array}{r}27\\ \times\ 5\end{array}$

4 $\begin{array}{r}36\\ \times\ 8\end{array}$ **8** $\begin{array}{r}53\\ \times\ 8\end{array}$

Work out

9 57 ÷ 3   **13** 85 ÷ 5

10 72 ÷ 2   **14** 84 ÷ 3

11 92 ÷ 4   **15** 76 ÷ 4

12 120 ÷ 8   **16** 86 ÷ 2

17 There are three classes in Year 4. Each class has 26 children. How many children are there in Year 4?

18 Sophie saves 5p coins. She has 90p. How many coins has she saved?

C

Work out

1 329 × 3   **9** 180 ÷ 5

2 146 × 2   **10** 267 ÷ 3

3 294 × 5   **11** 136 ÷ 2

4 153 × 6   **12** 148 ÷ 4

5 275 × 8   **13** 192 ÷ 8

6 428 × 7   **14** 210 ÷ 6

7 264 × 4   **15** 369 ÷ 9

8 138 × 9   **16** 161 ÷ 7

17 There are 6 apples in each packet. How many apples are there in 247 packets?

18 Jermain saves the same amount each month. In nine months he saves £585. How much does he save each month?

19 There are 128 nails in each packet. Martyn uses seven packets building a fence. How many nails has he used?

20 Each box holds the same number of tissues. Eight boxes contain 600 tissues altogether. How many tissues are there in each box?

TARGET   To solve word problems involving division mentally.

Examples

Thirty children are divided into 3 equal groups. How many children are there in each group?

$$30 \div 3 = 10$$

10 children in each group.

Each box holds 4 cakes. How many boxes are needed for 36 cakes?

$$36 \div 4 = 9$$

9 boxes are needed.

A

1. Dolly works five days each week. She works the same number of hours every day and 35 hours in a week altogether. How many hours does she work each day?

2. How many 10 cm lengths can be cut from 80 cm of string?

3. Alfie solves a jigsaw puzzle in 30 minutes. John does it in half the time. How long does John take to solve the puzzle?

4. How many triangles can be made from 18 straws?

5. Thirty PE mats are sorted into five equal piles. How many mats are there in each pile?

6. There are 28 children in a class. One quarter have fair hair. How many children in the class have fair hair?

B

1. Shelley has 32 fish. One quarter of the fish are red. How many red fish does she have?

2. Eight sandwiches are put onto each plate. How many plates are needed for 64 sandwiches?

3. Towels are made in equal numbers of pink, blue and green. How many pink towels are there if there are 60 towels altogether?

4. Lollipops cost 9p each. How many does Zack buy for 45p?

5. There are 48 children at a Gym Club. They are divided equally between the eight coaches. How many children are there in each group?

6. How many complete weeks are there in February in a year which is not a leap year?

C

1. Sixty pins are kept in each box. How many boxes are needed for 300 pins?

2. How many 20 g weights are needed to make 140 g?

3. A factory produces 240 cars. One eighth of the cars are sprayed red. How many cars are sprayed red?

4. Eggs are packed into boxes of 12. How many boxes are needed for sixty eggs?

5. There are 81 children in Year 3. They are divided equally into three classes. How many children are there in each class?

6. A garden centre sells plants in trays of nine? How many trays can be made from 72 plants?

TARGET To use ×/÷ facts to solve word problems.

Examples

I have 30p in 5p coins.
How many coins do I have?

$$30 \div 5 = 6$$

Answer *6 coins*

There are 4 balls in each box.
How many balls are there in 12 boxes?

$$12 \times 4 = 48$$

Answer *48 balls*

A

1. What is 9 times 2?
2. What is 3 multiplied by 10?
3. What is 7 times as big as 5?
4. How many 2s are there in 20?
5. What is 20 divided by 5?
6. What is 100 shared by 10?
7. I have five 5p coins. How much money do I have?
8. How much is eight 10p coins?
9. What is the value of six 2p coins?
10. How many 5p coins make 45p?
11. I have 50p. I have 10p coins only. How many coins do I have?
12. Each sweet weighs 10 g. What is the weight of four sweets?

B

1. What is 4 multiplied by 6?
2. What is 7 lots of 3?
3. How many 8s make 64?
4. What is six 5s?
5. How many is 36 shared by 4?
6. What is one third of 24?
7. How many days are there in 4 weeks?
8. There are eight eggs in each box. How many boxes can be filled from 48 eggs?
9. There are three flowers in each bunch. How many flowers are there in 12 bunches?
10. Thirty-two crayons are shared equally between 4 pots. How many crayons are there in each pot?
11. Five children sit at each table. How many children are there at eleven tables?
12. How many triangles can be made from 27 straws?

C

1. What number is nine times greater than 9?
2. How many 8s make 72?
3. Six 50 g weights are put on a scale. How much weight is this altogether?
4. I have 20p coins only. I have £1·60. How many coins do I have?
5. How many weeks are there in 56 days?
6. One card costs 30p. What do six cards cost?
7. Each plate has six cookies. How many cookies are there on 12 plates?
8. What is one ninth of 63?
9. One glass holds 200 ml. How many glasses can be filled from 1000 ml of drink?
10. What is seven multiplied by itself?
11. There are 40 rubber bands in one packet. How many bands are there in 5 packets?
12. What is ten times ten times ten?

TARGET   To write and calculate ×/÷ statements to solve word problems.

Examples

What is the product of 40 and 2?

$40 \times 2 = 80$

Answer *80*

3 coins of equal value make 15p. What is the coin?

$15 \div 3 = 5$

Answer *5p*

A

1. What is 7 groups of 4?
2. Find 9 multiplied by 2.
3. How many 3s make 18?
4. Share 50 by 10.
5. What is 8 times 5?
6. Divide 24 by 4.
7. Vicky has 5p coins only. She has 20p. How many coins does she have?
8. There are six eggs in each box. How many eggs are there in 5 boxes?
9. Ben writes 3 lines in 20 minutes. Damon writes eight times as many. How many lines does Damon write?
10. There are 36 footballs. A quarter of them are flat. How many of the balls are flat?

B

1. Find 11 lots of 8.
2. How many groups of 5 can be made from 35 children?
3. What is the product of 15 and 2?
4. What is 48 divided by 4?
5. What number is 3 times greater than 8?
6. There are 24 sweets in a packet. They are shared equally between six friends. How many do they have each?
7. Nine of the cows in a field are sitting down. Five times as many are standing up. How many cows are standing up?
8. A class of 27 children sit in groups of 3. How many children are in each group?
9. One quarter of the dogs in a dog show win a prize. There are 48 dogs at the show. How many win a prize?
10. Dulcie has 5 different wrapping papers and 8 different ribbons. How many different ways could she wrap a parcel?

C

1. How many days are there in eight weeks?
2. Which number, when multiplied by 4, gives an answer of 200?
3. What is half the product of 6 and 7?
4. Which number, when multiplied by itself, gives an answer of 81?
5. One in every five children in a school are in the choir. 40 children are in the choir. How many children are in the school?
6. Children pay half price to visit a zoo. The cost of 2 adult and 2 child tickets is £48. How much is one adult ticket?
7. Neil buys twelve boxes of 6 cakes each. The cakes are divided equally between 8 plates. How many cakes are on each plate?
8. How many minutes are there in 120 seconds?
9. A pie shop makes three different pastries and serves twelve different fillings. How many different pies are sold?

TARGET To write and calculate mathematical statements for ×/÷.

Examples

Find one third of 90 cm.	$90 \div 3 = 30$ Answer *30 cm*	What number is 4 times larger than 11?	$11 \times 4 = 44$ Answer *44*

A

1 What is 5 times 3?

2 Divide 40 by 5.

3 Multiply 2 by 8.

4 How many 4s make 20?

5 Find 7 groups of 10.

6 Share 24 by 8.

7 What is 9 lots of 5?

8 What is 4 multiplied by 6?

9 Divide 100 by 10.

10 What is 5 times as big as 6?

11 What is 20 divided by 2?

12 How much is seven 5ps?

13 What is 18 shared by 3?

15 How many 4s make 16?

15 Find 24 divided by 3?

16 What is 2 times 2 times 2?

B

1 What is 3 times 9?

2 What is the seventh multiple of:
   a) 4   b) 11?

3 Find one fifth of 60.

4 Multiply 30 by 4.

5 Find the product of 4 and 8.

6 What is 16 times greater than 2?

7 Five sweets weigh 100 g. What does one sweet weigh?

8 Aisha picks 36 apples. One in every four is rotten. How many apples are rotten?

9 A canteen serves 9 main meals and 3 desserts. How many 2-course meals are possible?

10 Which number, when multiplied by itself, gives an answer of 25?

11 Sixty children sit in three equal rows. How many children are there in each row?

12 Yasir has 4 jackets and 8 pairs of trousers. How many different outfits can he wear?

C

Look at the numbers in the box.

5	9	12	20	30

1 What is:
   a) the 4th multiple of the middle number
   b) the 8th multiple of the largest number
   c) the 21st multiple of the smallest number?

2 Multiply the two largest numbers.

3 Find the product of the three smallest numbers.

4 What number is twice as large as the second smallest number multiplied by itself?

5 Which number is ten times smaller than the second largest number multiplied by itself?

6 Ten different products can be made using pairs of the five numbers. Can you find them all?

7 Ten different products can be made using groups of three of the above numbers. Can you find them all?

TARGET   To solve 1-step and 2-step word problems.

Example

Max has six boxes of 4 tennis balls and 17 other loose balls. How many balls does he have altogether?

$6 \times 4 = 24$
$24 + 17 = 41$
Answer
Max has 41 balls altogether.

A

1. There are 22 slices of bread in one loaf. How many slices are there in three loaves?

2. In a library there are 17 men, 9 women and 20 children. How many people are in the library?

3. There are 53 books on the top shelf and 29 on the lower shelf. How many more books are on the top shelf than on the lower one?

4. Noah walks 2 km in 20 minutes. How far does he walk in one hour?

5. Zena works six hours a day for four days and eight hours on a fifth day. How many hours has she worked altogether?

6. Kane buys some sweets. Each sweet costs 5p. He pays 50p and is given 20p change. How many sweets does Kane buy?

B

1. Warren's shadow is 47 cm long. Imran's shadow is 38 cm longer. How long is Imran's shadow?

2. Fifty children travel home on the school bus. 18 get off at the first stop. A quarter of those still on the bus get off at the second stop. How many children are left on the bus?

3. A restaurant serves 24 main courses and five desserts. How many different two course meals are possible?

4. One half of a 1000 g bag of flour is used. A further 200 g is used. How much flour is left?

5. Cassie buys two oranges and a peach for 85p. Oranges cost 25p. What does the peach cost?

6. A hose uses 100 litres of water in ten minutes. How much water does it use in three minutes?

C

1. Derren's book has 140 pages. He has read a quarter of them. How many pages does he still have to read?

2. Cans of dog food cost 36p. How much do eight cans cost?

3. There are 227 children in the upper school and 79 fewer in the lower school. How many children are there in the whole school?

4. Adult bus tickets cost £2.50. Children travel half price. What is the cost of one adult and three child tickets?

5. One tea bag weighs 3 g. A box of 80 tea bags weighs 265 g. What does the box weigh?

TARGET To find the relevant information to solve word problems.

Examples

Barry's book has 50 pages. 17 of the pages have pictures. Ian's book is 12 pages longer. How long is Ian's book?

50 + 12 = 62

Answer *Ian's book is 62 pages long.*
17 pages have pictures is not relevant.

Tania's book has 50 pages. She reads 16 pages. She reads another 11 pages. How many pages are left?

50 − 16 = 34

34 − 11 = 23

Answer *23 pages are left.*

A

1 There are 24 children on a bus. 20 people are sitting upstairs. 17 of the passengers are adults. How many people are on the bus?

2 There are 20 biscuits in a packet. A quarter are eaten. How many are left?

3 The chairs in a classroom are put into three stacks of six chairs and one stack of five. How many chairs are there in the room?

4 There are 32 chocolates in a box. 18 are milk chocolate. 12 have a hard centre. How many are not milk chocolate?

5 There are 14 boys and 13 girls in Class 3. They sit in three equal rows. How many children are in each row?

B

1 Thirteen less men than women work in a school. 28 women work there. How many adults work in the school altogether?

2 There are four cakes in each packet and 20 packets in each box. How many cakes are there in five boxes?

3 Books cost £5. A shop has an offer: *Buy one get one half price.* How much does Ann pay for two books?

4 There are 100 marbles in a jar. 28 are red. 17 are green. How many are not red?

5 There are eight teams of six players at a football tournament. There are equal numbers of boys and girls taking part. How many players are there at the tournament?

C

1 There are six 90 g doughnuts in each box. The box weighs 60 g. What is the total weight of the box and doughnuts?

2 There are 83 children and 39 adults at an outdoor swimming pool. 74 people are swimming. How many people are at the pool?

3 Joe buys three apples and a banana for 70p altogether. Apples cost 15p. What does the banana cost?

4 There are 124 horses in a field. Half the horses are brown. 38 horses go into the stables. How many are left on the field?

TARGET To solve number problems mentally.

Examples Find a pair of numbers with:

 1 a total of 30
   a difference of 8
   Answer *11, 19*

2 a product of 36
   a sum of 15
   Answer *3, 12*

A

Find the number.

1 between 10 and 20
   the sum of its digits is 8

2 between 40 and 50
   its digits have a difference of 5

3 below 50
   its digits multiplied together make 10

4 between 31 and 39
   a multiple of 6

5 I think of a number.
   I add 17.
   The answer is 22.
   What is my number?

6 I think of a number.
   I double it.
   The answer is 14.
   What is my number?

7 I think of a number.
   I take away 10.
   The answer is 58.
   What is my number?

8 I think of a number.
   I divide by 4.
   The answer is 9.
   What is my number?

Copy and complete.

9 39 + ☐ = 50

10 74 − ☐ = 68

B

Find the number.

1 between 50 and 100
   its digits have a total of 11 and a difference of 7

2 between 40 and 70
   a multiple of 9
   an even number

3 I think of a number.
   I halve it.
   I add 8.
   The answer is 12.
   What is my number?

4 I think of a number.
   I multiply by 5.
   I take away 2.
   The answer is 43.
   What is my number?

Find the pair of numbers with:

5 a total of 20
   a difference of 4

6 a total of 50
   a difference of 12

7 a sum of 12
   a product of 32

8 a sum of 11
   a product of 30

Copy and complete.

9 ☐ + 30 = 100

10 28 ÷ ☐ = 4

C

Find the 2-digit number.

1 an even number
   its digits have a total of 15 and a difference of 3

2 an odd number
   its digits have a product of 40

3 I think of a number.
   I subtract 4.
   I multiply by 5.
   The answer is 70.
   What is my number?

4 I think of a number.
   I divide by 6.
   I add 20.
   The answer is 32.
   What is my number?

Find the pair of numbers with:

5 a sum of 16
   a product of 48

6 a sum of 12
   a product of 27

7 a sum of 20
   a product of 36

8 a sum of 35
   a product of 150

Copy and complete.

9 ☐ + 11 = 105

10 86 − ☐ = 49

TARGET To identify and name unit and non-unit fractions.

Examples

UNIT FRACTION

$\frac{1}{8}$

one eighth is shaded

NON-UNIT FRACTION

$\frac{5}{6}$

five sixths is shaded

Here are some words you may need.

$\frac{1}{2}$ half	$\frac{1}{6}$ sixth	$\frac{1}{10}$ tenth
$\frac{1}{3}$ third	$\frac{1}{7}$ seventh	$\frac{1}{11}$ eleventh
$\frac{1}{4}$ quarter	$\frac{1}{8}$ eighth	$\frac{1}{12}$ twelfth
$\frac{1}{5}$ fifth	$\frac{1}{9}$ ninth	

A

What fraction of each diagram is yellow?

 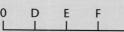 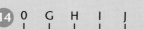

Write the fraction shown by each letter.

11 0 ____ A ____ 1

12 0 ____ B ____ C ____ 1

13 0 ____ D ____ E ____ F ____ 1

14 0 ____ G ____ H ____ I ____ J ____ 1

B

What fraction of each diagram is shaded orange?

Write the fraction shown by each letter.

9 0 A ____ B ____ 1

10 0 C ____ D ____ 1

11 0 E ____ F ____ 1

12 Draw fraction lines like those above to show:

a) $\frac{1}{5}, \frac{3}{5}$ c) $\frac{1}{10}, \frac{5}{10}$

b) $\frac{1}{8}, \frac{7}{8}$ d) $\frac{1}{12}, \frac{8}{12}$

C

Write the equivalent (equal) fractions shown by the letters for each pair of number lines.

1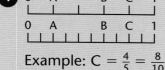

Example: $C = \frac{4}{5} = \frac{8}{10}$

2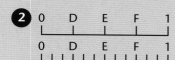

3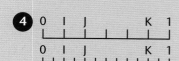

4 0 I J ____ K 1

Use squared paper. Draw a pair of diagrams to show these equivalent fractions.

5 $\frac{1}{2} = \frac{4}{8}$

6 $\frac{2}{3} = \frac{8}{12}$

7 $\frac{1}{4} = \frac{4}{16}$

8 $\frac{3}{5} = \frac{9}{15}$

TARGET   To count up and down in tenths.

Examples

Start at $\frac{5}{10}$. Count on $\frac{3}{10}$.

$$\frac{5}{10}, \frac{6}{10}, \frac{7}{10}, \frac{8}{10}$$

Answer $\frac{8}{10}$

Start at 1. Count back $\frac{4}{10}$.

$$1 = \frac{10}{10}, \frac{9}{10}, \frac{8}{10}, \frac{7}{10}, \frac{6}{10}$$

Answer $\frac{6}{10}$

A

What fraction of each shape is shaded?

1   5

2   6

3   7

4   8

9 Start at 0.
Count in halves to 3.

10 Start at 5.
Count on in quarters to 7.

11 Start at 10.
Count back in halves to 6.

12 Start at $1\frac{3}{4}$.
Count back in quarters to 0.

B

Write the fraction shown:
a) in words
b) in figures.

1   3

2   4

5 Write the fraction shown by each letter:
a) in words
b) in figures.

0 A   B   C   1

Count on or back in tenths.

6 Start at two tenths.
Count on four tenths.

7 Start at seven tenths.
Count back three tenths.

8 Start at three tenths.
Count on six tenths.

9 Start at one.
Count back seven tenths.

10 Start at one tenth.
Count on nine tenths.

C

What fraction of each diagram is:
a) green   b) white?

Write your answer in both figures and words.

1   6

2   7

3   8

4   9

5   10

Write the first six numbers.

11 Start at 0.
Count on in eighths.

12 Start at 1.
Count back in ninths.

13 Start at three twelfths.
Count on in twelfths.

14 Start at 1.
Count back in sixths.

TARGET To connect tenths to decimal measures and division by 10.

Examples

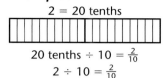

2 = 20 tenths

$20 \text{ tenths} \div 10 = \frac{2}{10}$

$2 \div 10 = \frac{2}{10}$

Tenths can be written as decimals.

$2 \text{ tenths} = 0.2$

$\frac{7}{10} = 0.7$

Decimals are used to show measures.

$5 \text{ cm} \div 10 = \frac{5}{10} \text{ cm} = 0.5 \text{ cm}$

$3 \text{ kg} \div 10 = \frac{3}{10} \text{ kg} = 0.3 \text{ kg}$

A

Copy and complete.

1. 3 = ☐ tenths
2. 7 = ☐ tenths
3. 4 = ☐ tenths
4. 9 = ☐ tenths
5. 1 = ☐ tenths
6. 6 = ☐ tenths

Copy and complete by writing a fraction.

7. 40 tenths ÷ 10 = ☐
8. 20 tenths ÷ 10 = ☐
9. 50 tenths ÷ 10 = ☐
10. 80 tenths ÷ 10 = ☐
11. 60 tenths ÷ 10 = ☐
12. 30 tenths ÷ 10 = ☐

Write the answer as a fraction.

13. 6 ÷ 10
14. 1 ÷ 10
15. 7 ÷ 10
16. 5 ÷ 10
17. 2 ÷ 10
18. 9 ÷ 10
19. 3 ÷ 10
20. 8 ÷ 10

B

Copy and complete by writing a fraction.

1. 2 cm ÷ 10 = ☐ cm
2. 9 kg ÷ 10 = ☐ kg
3. 4 m ÷ 10 = ☐ m
4. 7 km ÷ 10 = ☐ km
5. 1 cm ÷ 10 = ☐ cm
6. 5 kg ÷ 10 = ☐ kg
7. 8 m ÷ 10 = ☐ m
8. 3 km ÷ 10 = ☐ km

Copy and complete by writing a decimal.

9. 6 cm ÷ 10 = ☐ cm
10. 1 kg ÷ 10 = ☐ kg
11. 9 m ÷ 10 = ☐ m
12. 5 km ÷ 10 = ☐ km
13. 4 cm ÷ 10 = ☐ cm
14. 7 kg ÷ 10 = ☐ kg
15. 2 m ÷ 10 = ☐ m
16. 8 km ÷ 10 = ☐ km

C

Copy and complete by writing a fraction.

Example: $37 \text{ m} \div 10 = 3\frac{7}{10} \text{ m}$

1. 28 m ÷ 10 = ☐ m
2. 65 kg ÷ 10 = ☐ kg
3. 53 cm ÷ 10 = ☐ cm
4. 86 km ÷ 10 = ☐ km
5. 34 m ÷ 10 = ☐ m
6. 79 kg ÷ 10 = ☐ kg
7. 42 cm ÷ 10 = ☐ cm
8. 17 km ÷ 10 = ☐ km

Copy and complete by writing a decimal measure.

9. 19 m ÷ 10 = ☐ m
10. 54 kg ÷ 10 = ☐ kg
11. 45 cm ÷ 10 = ☐ cm
12. 72 km ÷ 10 = ☐ km
13. 87 m ÷ 10 = ☐ m
14. 21 kg ÷ 10 = ☐ kg
15. 96 cm ÷ 10 = ☐ cm
16. 33 km ÷ 10 = ☐ km

TARGET To find fractions of a set of objects and quantities.

Examples

$\frac{1}{3}$ of 12 = 4

$\frac{1}{4}$ of 28 = 28 ÷ 4
$= 7$

$\frac{3}{4}$ of 28 = (28 ÷ 4) × 3
$= 7 × 3$
$= 21$

A

Use the diagram to help you find:

1. $\frac{1}{2}$ of 8
2. $\frac{1}{4}$ of 8
3. $\frac{1}{3}$ of 15
4. $\frac{1}{5}$ of 15
5. $\frac{1}{2}$ of 6
6. $\frac{1}{3}$ of 6
7. $\frac{1}{3}$ of 12
8. $\frac{1}{4}$ of 12
9. $\frac{1}{2}$ of 18
10. $\frac{1}{3}$ of 18
11. $\frac{1}{6}$ of 18
12. $\frac{1}{4}$ of 20
13. $\frac{1}{5}$ of 20
14. $\frac{1}{2}$ of 20
15. Draw a diagram to help you find:
    a) $\frac{1}{4}$ of 16
    b) $\frac{1}{8}$ of 16
    c) $\frac{1}{2}$ of 16

B

Copy and complete.

1. $\frac{1}{3}$ of 24 = 24 ÷ 3
   = ☐
2. $\frac{1}{5}$ of 30 = ☐ ÷ 5
   = ☐
3. $\frac{1}{2}$ of 18 = 18 ÷ ☐
   = ☐
4. $\frac{1}{4}$ of 32 = ☐ ÷ 4
   = ☐
5. $\frac{1}{10}$ of 50 = ☐ ÷ ☐
   = ☐
6. $\frac{1}{8}$ of 24 = ☐ ÷ ☐
   = ☐

Work out

7. $\frac{1}{5}$ of 25 cm
8. $\frac{1}{2}$ of 40 g
9. $\frac{1}{4}$ of 24 litres
10. $\frac{1}{3}$ of 30p
11. $\frac{1}{10}$ of 70 m
12. $\frac{1}{6}$ of 30 seconds
13. $\frac{1}{3}$ of 27 kg
14. $\frac{1}{5}$ of 40 mm
15. $\frac{1}{8}$ of £32
16. $\frac{1}{4}$ of 60 minutes

C

Copy and complete.

1. $\frac{3}{4}$ of 16 = (16 ÷ 4) × 3
   = ☐ × 3
   = ☐
2. $\frac{9}{10}$ of 50 = (50 ÷ 10) × 9
   = ☐ × ☐
   = ☐
3. $\frac{5}{6}$ of 36 = (36 ÷ 6) × 5
   = ☐ × ☐
   = ☐
4. $\frac{3}{8}$ of 40 = (40 ÷ 8) × ☐
   = ☐ × ☐
   = ☐

Work out

5. $\frac{2}{3}$ of £24
6. $\frac{3}{5}$ of 50p
7. $\frac{7}{10}$ of 80 m
8. $\frac{4}{9}$ of 45 kg
9. $\frac{5}{6}$ of 5·4 cm
10. $\frac{7}{8}$ of £16
11. $\frac{3}{4}$ of 36p
12. $\frac{6}{7}$ of 210 m
13. $\frac{4}{5}$ of 100 g
14. $\frac{2}{9}$ of £7·20

TARGET   To find fractions of a set of objects and amounts.

Examples

$\frac{1}{3}$ of 18 = 6

$\frac{2}{3}$ of 18 = 12

$\frac{1}{6}$ of 18 = 3

$\frac{5}{6}$ of 18 = 15

$\frac{1}{4}$ of 40 = 40 ÷ 4
= 10

$\frac{3}{4}$ of 40 = (40 ÷ 4) × 3
= 10 × 3
= 30

A

Use the squares to help you find:

1. $\frac{1}{2}$ of 6
2. $\frac{1}{3}$ of 6

3. $\frac{1}{3}$ of 15
4. $\frac{1}{5}$ of 15

5. $\frac{1}{2}$ of 12
6. $\frac{1}{3}$ of 12
7. $\frac{1}{4}$ of 12

8. $\frac{1}{4}$ of 20
9. $\frac{1}{5}$ of 20
10. $\frac{1}{2}$ of 20

11. $\frac{1}{4}$ of 24
12. $\frac{1}{6}$ of 24
13. $\frac{1}{2}$ of 24

Find

14. $\frac{1}{2}$ of 18
15. $\frac{1}{3}$ of 9
16. $\frac{1}{5}$ of 10
17. $\frac{1}{10}$ of 100
18. $\frac{1}{4}$ of 32
19. $\frac{1}{6}$ of 30

B

Look at the squares in Section A. Work out

1. a) $\frac{1}{3}$ of 6
   b) $\frac{2}{3}$ of 6
2. a) $\frac{1}{5}$ of 15
   b) $\frac{3}{5}$ of 15
3. a) $\frac{1}{4}$ of 12
   b) $\frac{3}{4}$ of 12
4. a) $\frac{1}{5}$ of 20
   b) $\frac{4}{5}$ of 20
5. a) $\frac{1}{6}$ of 24
   b) $\frac{5}{6}$ of 24
6. a) $\frac{1}{3}$ of 24
   b) $\frac{2}{3}$ of 24

Find $\frac{1}{5}$ of:

7. 30
8. 25
9. 50
10. 35

Find $\frac{1}{4}$ of:

15. 8
16. 16
17. 28
18. 36

Find $\frac{1}{3}$ of:

11. 18
12. 60
13. 36
14. 27

Find $\frac{1}{10}$ of:

19. 40
20. 120
21. 300
22. 750

C

Find

1. $\frac{3}{4}$ of 24
2. $\frac{2}{3}$ of 21
3. $\frac{4}{5}$ of 45
4. $\frac{1}{8}$ of 48
5. $\frac{7}{10}$ of 60
6. $\frac{5}{8}$ of 32
7. $\frac{3}{10}$ of 200
8. $\frac{2}{3}$ of 60
9. $\frac{3}{4}$ of 100
10. $\frac{2}{5}$ of 100
11. $\frac{9}{10}$ of 500
12. $\frac{1}{100}$ of 1000

13. There are 30 children in a class. Nine tenths are present. How many children are absent?

14. There are 24 bottles in a crate. Two thirds are empty. How many bottles are not empty?

15. There are 56 pills in a packet. Three eighths have been taken. How many are left?

TARGET To find fractions of quantities by repeated halving.

Examples

$\frac{1}{2}$ of 16 = 8 $\frac{1}{4}$ of 16 = 4 $\frac{1}{8}$ of 16 = 2 $\frac{1}{2}$ of £2·40 = £1·20

⚫⚫⚫⚫⚫⚫⚫⚫   ⚫⚫⚫⚫ ⚫⚫⚫⚫   ⚫⚫ ⚫⚫ ⚫⚫ ⚫⚫ $\frac{1}{4}$ of £2·40 = £0·60
⚫⚫⚫⚫⚫⚫⚫⚫   ⚫⚫⚫⚫ ⚫⚫⚫⚫   ⚫⚫ ⚫⚫ ⚫⚫ ⚫⚫ $\frac{1}{8}$ of £2·40 = £0·30

A

Copy and complete.

1. $\frac{1}{2}$ of 12 counters is ☐.
   $\frac{1}{4}$ of 12 counters is ☐.

2. $\frac{1}{2}$ of ☐ counters is 4.
   $\frac{1}{4}$ of ☐ counters is 2.

3. $\frac{1}{2}$ of 20 counters is ☐.
   $\frac{1}{4}$ of 20 counters is ☐.

4. $\frac{1}{2}$ of ☐ counters is 8.
   $\frac{1}{4}$ of ☐ counters is 4.

Copy and complete by writing a fraction in each box.

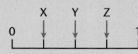

5. X shows ☐

6. Y shows ☐

7. Z shows ☐

Copy and complete by writing a letter in each box.

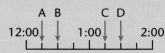

8. ☐ shows half past 12

9. ☐ shows quarter past 1

10. ☐ shows quarter past 12

11. ☐ shows half past 1

B

Find

1. $\frac{1}{4}$ of 80p

2. $\frac{1}{8}$ of 40p

3. $\frac{1}{4}$ of £2

4. $\frac{1}{8}$ of £16

5. $\frac{1}{4}$ of 60 cm

6. $\frac{1}{8}$ of 48 cm

7. $\frac{1}{4}$ of £36

8. $\frac{1}{8}$ of £2

9. Copy and complete by writing a fraction in each box.

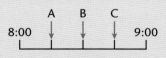

A shows ☐ past 8.

B shows ☐ past 8.

C shows ☐ to 9.

10. How much is:
    a) half of 200 g
    b) a quarter of 200 g
    c) an eighth of 200 g?

11. How much is:
    a) half of 56 litres
    b) a quarter of 56 litres
    c) an eighth of 56 litres?

C

Find

1. $\frac{1}{4}$ of £5

2. $\frac{1}{8}$ of £6

3. $\frac{1}{4}$ of 140 m

4. $\frac{1}{8}$ of 64 m

5. $\frac{1}{3}$ of 12 counters

6. $\frac{1}{6}$ of 12 counters

7. $\frac{1}{5}$ of 40p

8. $\frac{1}{10}$ of 40p

9. $\frac{1}{4}$ of 48 cm

10. $\frac{3}{4}$ of 48 cm

11. $\frac{1}{4}$ of 200 g

12. $\frac{3}{4}$ of 200 g

13. Write the time shown by each letter.

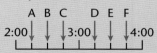

14. How much is:
    a) half of £10
    b) a quarter of £10
    c) an eighth of £10?

15. How much is:
    a) $\frac{1}{3}$ of 180 m
    b) $\frac{1}{6}$ of 180 m
    c) $\frac{1}{12}$ of 180 m?

TARGET   To recognise and show equivalent fractions.

Equivalent fractions are fractions that look different but are the same.

Examples

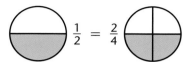 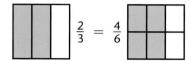

A

Use the number lines to complete the equivalent fractions.

1. $\frac{1}{4} = \frac{\square}{8}$ 3. $\frac{3}{4} = \frac{\square}{8}$

2. $\frac{1}{2} = \frac{\square}{8}$ 4. $\frac{2}{4} = \frac{\square}{8}$

Write the equivalent fractions shown in each pair of diagrams.

5.

6.

7.

8.

Draw a pair of diagrams to show:

9. $\frac{1}{2} = \frac{5}{10}$ 11. $\frac{1}{2} = \frac{3}{6}$

10. $\frac{1}{3} = \frac{3}{9}$ 12. $\frac{3}{4} = \frac{6}{8}$

B

Write the equivalent fractions shown in each pair of diagrams.

1.

2.

3.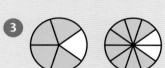

4.

5.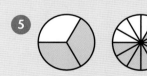

6.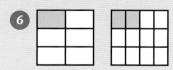

Draw a pair of diagrams to show:

7. $\frac{3}{4} = \frac{9}{12}$ 9. $\frac{2}{5} = \frac{4}{10}$

8. $\frac{2}{3} = \frac{6}{9}$ 10. $\frac{5}{6} = \frac{10}{12}$

C

Copy and complete.

1. $\frac{1}{2} = \frac{\square}{6}$ 7. $\frac{3}{5} = \frac{\square}{100}$

2. $\frac{3}{4} = \frac{\square}{16}$ 8. $\frac{9}{10} = \frac{\square}{50}$

3. $\frac{4}{5} = \frac{\square}{10}$ 9. $\frac{2}{7} = \frac{\square}{14}$

4. $\frac{7}{10} = \frac{\square}{100}$ 10. $\frac{3}{4} = \frac{\square}{20}$

5. $\frac{2}{3} = \frac{\square}{15}$ 11. $\frac{11}{25} = \frac{\square}{100}$

6. $\frac{3}{8} = \frac{\square}{16}$ 12. $\frac{2}{3} = \frac{\square}{18}$

Write the next five fractions in these chains.

13. $\frac{1}{2} = \frac{2}{4} = \frac{3}{6}$

14. $\frac{1}{3} = \frac{2}{6} = \frac{3}{9}$

15. $\frac{3}{4} = \frac{6}{8} = \frac{9}{12}$

16. $\frac{2}{5} = \frac{4}{10} = \frac{6}{15}$

Write $>$, $<$ or $=$ in each box.

17. $\frac{1}{2} \square \frac{6}{10}$ 21. $\frac{1}{3} \square \frac{2}{9}$

18. $\frac{2}{3} \square \frac{3}{6}$ 22. $\frac{2}{6} \square \frac{4}{12}$

19. $\frac{2}{5} \square \frac{4}{10}$ 23. $\frac{1}{2} \square \frac{5}{12}$

20. $\frac{1}{4} \square \frac{3}{16}$ 24. $\frac{3}{8} \square \frac{7}{16}$

EQUIVALENT FRACTIONS 2 68

TARGET   To recognise and show equivalent fractions.

Example
Write the fraction shown in two different ways.

   $\frac{1}{2} = \frac{6}{12}$

A

Write the fraction of each shape which is shaded?

1   5

2   6

3   7

4   8

Copy and complete by writing $\frac{1}{2}$ or $\frac{1}{4}$ in the box.

9    $\frac{6}{12} = \square$

10    $\frac{2}{8} = \square$

11    $\frac{4}{8} = \square$

12    $\frac{3}{12} = \square$

B

Copy and complete the equivalent fractions.

1    $\frac{\square}{10} = \frac{1}{5}$

2    $\frac{\square}{6} = \frac{1}{3}$

3    $\frac{4}{12} = \frac{1}{\square}$

4    $\frac{4}{8} = \frac{1}{\square}$

Write the fraction shown in two different ways.

5   7

6   8

9 Draw a diagram to show each pair of equivalent fractions.

a) $\frac{1}{3} = \frac{3}{9}$

b) $\frac{1}{2} = \frac{6}{12}$

c) $\frac{1}{6} = \frac{2}{12}$

C

Copy and complete the equivalent fractions.

1    $\frac{6}{8} = \frac{\square}{4}$

2    $\frac{6}{9} = \frac{\square}{3}$

3    $\frac{4}{10} = \frac{\square}{5}$

4    $\frac{9}{12} = \frac{\square}{4}$

Write the fraction shown in two different ways.

5   7

6   8

9 Draw a diagram to show each pair of equivalent fractions.

a) $\frac{3}{5} = \frac{6}{10}$

b) $\frac{5}{6} = \frac{10}{12}$

c) $\frac{3}{4} = \frac{9}{12}$

TARGET To recognise pairs of fractions that add up to 1.

Examples

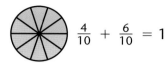 $\frac{4}{10} + \frac{6}{10} = 1$  $\frac{11}{12} + \frac{1}{12} = 1$

A

Use the diagram to complete the pair of fractions that make one whole one.

1 $1 = \dfrac{\square}{2} + \dfrac{\square}{2}$

2 $1 = \dfrac{\square}{4} + \dfrac{\square}{4}$

3 $1 = \dfrac{\square}{4} + \dfrac{\square}{4}$

4 $1 = \dfrac{\square}{3} + \dfrac{\square}{3}$

Copy and complete.

5 one = ☐ thirds

6 one = ☐ halves

7 one = ☐ quarters

8 one = ☐ tenths

9 One half of a cake has been eaten. What fraction of the cake is left?

10 One quarter of a fence has been painted. What fraction of the fence has not been painted?

B

Use the diagram to complete each pair of fractions that make one whole one.

1 $1 = \dfrac{\square}{8} + \dfrac{\square}{8}$

2 $1 = \dfrac{\square}{5} + \dfrac{\square}{5}$

3   **6**

4   **7**

5   **8**

9 Seven eighths of a box of corn flakes has been used. What fraction is left?

10 Three twelfths of a bar of chocolate is eaten. What fraction has not been eaten?

11 One ninth of tape is used. What fraction is left?

C

Copy and complete.

1 $1 = \dfrac{4}{10} + \square$

2 $1 = \dfrac{2}{5} + \square$

3 $1 = \dfrac{5}{12} + \square$

4 $1 = \dfrac{6}{8} + \square$

5 $1 = \dfrac{3}{7} + \square$

6 $1 = \dfrac{9}{11} + \square$

7 $1 = \dfrac{4}{6} + \square$

8 $1 = \dfrac{2}{9} + \square$

9 $1 = \dfrac{1}{11} + \square$

10 $1 = \dfrac{7}{10} + \square$

11 One eighth of a bottle of milk is used. A further two eighths is used. What fraction is left?

12 Two fifths of a pizza is eaten on Monday. Another two fifths is eaten on Tuesday. What fraction of the pizza is left?

TARGET   To add and subtract fractions with the same denominator.

Adding fractions with the same bottom number (denominator).
Add the top numbers (numerators) and put the answer over the same denominator.

Example   A bar of chocolate has 8 squares
3 are eaten. 2 more are eaten.
What fraction of the bar has been eaten?

 $\frac{3}{8} + \frac{2}{8} = \frac{5}{8}$

Answer: $\frac{5}{8}$ *has been eaten.*

Subtracting fractions with the same denominator.
Subtract the second numerator from the first and put the answer over the same denominator.

Example   A pizza has 10 slices.
7 slices are left. 3 more are eaten.
What fraction of the pizza is left?

 $\frac{7}{10} - \frac{3}{10} = \frac{4}{10}$

Answer: $\frac{4}{10}$ *is left.*

A
Work out.

1. $\frac{1}{4} + \frac{1}{4} = \frac{\square}{4}$

2. $\frac{2}{6} + \frac{3}{6} = \frac{\square}{6}$

3. $\frac{6}{10} + \frac{3}{10} = \frac{\square}{10}$

4. $\frac{5}{8} + \frac{1}{8} = \frac{\square}{8}$

5. $\frac{2}{5} + \frac{1}{5} = \frac{\square}{5}$

6. $\frac{4}{11} + \frac{5}{11} = \frac{\square}{11}$

7. $\frac{2}{3} - \frac{1}{3} = \frac{\square}{3}$

8. $\frac{6}{8} - \frac{5}{8} = \frac{\square}{8}$

9. $\frac{4}{5} - \frac{2}{5} = \frac{\square}{5}$

10. $\frac{7}{10} - \frac{5}{10} = \frac{\square}{10}$

11. $\frac{3}{4} - \frac{2}{4} = \frac{\square}{4}$

12. $\frac{11}{12} - \frac{7}{12} = \frac{\square}{12}$

B
Work out

1. $\frac{1}{9} + \frac{6}{9}$

2. $\frac{3}{5} + \frac{1}{5}$

3. $\frac{1}{8} + \frac{4}{8}$

4. $\frac{6}{10} + \frac{2}{10}$

5. $\frac{2}{7} + \frac{4}{7}$

6. $\frac{4}{12} + \frac{5}{12}$

7. $\frac{7}{8} - \frac{5}{8}$

8. $\frac{4}{4} - \frac{3}{4}$

9. $\frac{6}{10} - \frac{3}{10}$

10. $\frac{5}{7} - \frac{4}{7}$

11. $\frac{6}{6} - \frac{4}{6}$

12. $\frac{9}{11} - \frac{2}{11}$

Copy and complete.

13. $\frac{1}{10} + \frac{\square}{10} = \frac{9}{10}$

14. $\frac{5}{12} + \frac{\square}{12} = \frac{7}{12}$

15. $\frac{\square}{9} + \frac{3}{9} = \frac{8}{9}$

16. $\frac{11}{11} - \frac{\square}{11} = \frac{3}{11}$

17. $\frac{7}{8} - \frac{\square}{8} = \frac{4}{8}$

18. $\frac{9}{10} - \frac{\square}{10} = \frac{5}{10}$

C
Copy and complete.

1. $\frac{3}{10} + \frac{\square}{10} + \frac{1}{10} = \frac{8}{10}$

2. $\frac{1}{6} + \frac{1}{6} + \frac{\square}{6} = \frac{5}{6}$

3. $\frac{\square}{9} + \frac{2}{9} + \frac{3}{9} = \frac{7}{9}$

4. $\frac{1}{7} + \frac{4}{7} + \frac{\square}{7} = 1$

5. $\frac{3}{11} + \frac{\square}{11} + \frac{3}{11} = \frac{10}{11}$

6. $\frac{\square}{12} + \frac{2}{12} + \frac{1}{12} = \frac{9}{12}$

7. $\frac{7}{8} - \frac{1}{8} - \frac{\square}{8} = \frac{1}{8}$

8. $1 - \frac{\square}{5} - \frac{2}{5} = \frac{2}{5}$

9. $1 - \frac{4}{9} - \frac{\square}{9} = \frac{2}{9}$

10. $\frac{11}{12} - \frac{\square}{12} - \frac{2}{12} = \frac{4}{12}$

11. $1 - \frac{2}{10} - \frac{\square}{10} = \frac{1}{10}$

12. $\frac{9}{11} - \frac{\square}{11} - \frac{5}{11} = \frac{2}{11}$

TARGET   To compare and order fractions.

The smaller the bottom number, the larger the fraction.

Example   A bar of chocolate
has 8 squares $\frac{1}{2}$ = 4 squares $\frac{1}{4}$ = 2 squares $\frac{1}{8}$ = 1 square

The smaller the top number, the smaller the fraction.

Example   A pizza has
10 equal slices. $\frac{1}{10}$ = 1 slice $\frac{2}{10}$ = 2 slices $\frac{4}{10}$ = 4 slices

---

A

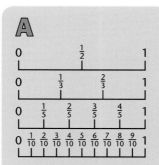

Look at the number lines. Write down if each fraction is:

a) greater than one half

b) less than one half.

1) $\frac{4}{5}$ 5) $\frac{2}{5}$

2) $\frac{3}{10}$ 6) $\frac{2}{3}$

3) $\frac{1}{3}$ 7) $\frac{4}{10}$

4) $\frac{7}{10}$ 8) $\frac{3}{5}$

Which fraction is larger?

9) $\frac{1}{3}$ or $\frac{1}{4}$ 13) $\frac{1}{4}$ or $\frac{3}{4}$

10) $\frac{1}{5}$ or $\frac{1}{3}$ 14) $\frac{3}{5}$ or $\frac{2}{5}$

11) $\frac{1}{10}$ or $\frac{1}{5}$ 15) $\frac{2}{3}$ or $\frac{1}{3}$

12) $\frac{1}{4}$ or $\frac{1}{10}$ 16) $\frac{3}{10}$ or $\frac{7}{10}$

B

Write the larger of each pair of fractions.

1) $\frac{2}{6}$ $\frac{5}{6}$ 7) $\frac{1}{8}$ $\frac{1}{5}$

2) $\frac{3}{11}$ $\frac{1}{11}$ 8) $\frac{5}{6}$ $\frac{5}{7}$

3) $\frac{5}{8}$ $\frac{7}{8}$ 9) $\frac{2}{5}$ $\frac{2}{3}$

4) $\frac{1}{9}$ $\frac{4}{9}$ 10) $\frac{8}{9}$ $\frac{8}{11}$

5) $\frac{11}{12}$ $\frac{7}{12}$ 11) $\frac{3}{4}$ $\frac{3}{8}$

6) $\frac{4}{7}$ $\frac{3}{7}$ 12) $\frac{7}{12}$ $\frac{7}{10}$

Write in order, smallest first.

13) $\frac{2}{5}$, $\frac{4}{5}$, $\frac{1}{5}$

14) $\frac{1}{11}$, $\frac{1}{2}$, $\frac{1}{3}$

15) $\frac{7}{12}$, $\frac{5}{12}$, $\frac{10}{12}$

16) $\frac{3}{5}$, $\frac{3}{7}$, $\frac{3}{6}$

17) $\frac{6}{8}$, $\frac{3}{8}$, $\frac{1}{8}$

18) $\frac{5}{9}$, $\frac{5}{12}$, $\frac{5}{8}$

C

Look at the number lines. Write down the larger of each pair of fractions.

1) $\frac{1}{4}$ $\frac{1}{6}$ 5) $\frac{3}{4}$ $\frac{8}{12}$

2) $\frac{3}{8}$ $\frac{5}{12}$ 6) $\frac{5}{8}$ $\frac{4}{6}$

3) $\frac{3}{4}$ $\frac{7}{8}$ 7) $\frac{3}{8}$ $\frac{1}{4}$

4) $\frac{2}{6}$ $\frac{3}{12}$ 8) $\frac{9}{12}$ $\frac{5}{6}$

Write in order, smallest first.

9) $\frac{1}{2}$, $\frac{1}{4}$, $\frac{1}{5}$

10) $\frac{3}{4}$, $\frac{3}{8}$, $\frac{1}{2}$

11) $\frac{4}{5}$, $\frac{1}{2}$, $\frac{4}{6}$

12) $\frac{1}{2}$, $\frac{5}{8}$, $\frac{5}{12}$

13) $\frac{2}{5}$, $\frac{2}{10}$, $\frac{1}{2}$

14) $\frac{7}{12}$, $\frac{1}{2}$, $\frac{4}{10}$

TARGET   To use a range of scales to measure weight.

Work out the measurement shown by each arrow.

A

1. kg: 0 2 4 6 8

2. g: 0 10 20 30 40

3. g: 0 200 400 600 800

4. kg: 30 40 50 60 70

5. g: 0 20 40 60 80 100

6. g: 0 200 400 600 800 1000

7. kg: 2 4 6 8 10

8. kg: 20 30 40 50

9. g: 400 500 600 700 800

B

1. kg: 0 1 2 3 4

2. g: 0 50 100 150 200

3. g: 0 100 200 300 400

4. kg: 20 40 60 80

5. g: 0 40 80 120 160 200

6. g: 0 30 60 90 120 150

7. kg: 24 28 32 36 40

8. kg: 5 6 7 8 9 10

9. g: 150 200 250 300 350 400

C

1. kg: 0 1 2

2. g: 0 120 240

3. g: 0 25 50

4. kg: 0 1 2

5. g: 0 25 50 75 100

6. kg: 0 5 10

7. kg: 2 3 4

8. g: 500 600 700

9. kg: 37 38 39

TARGET To use a range of scales to measure capacity.

Work out the measurement shown by each arrow.

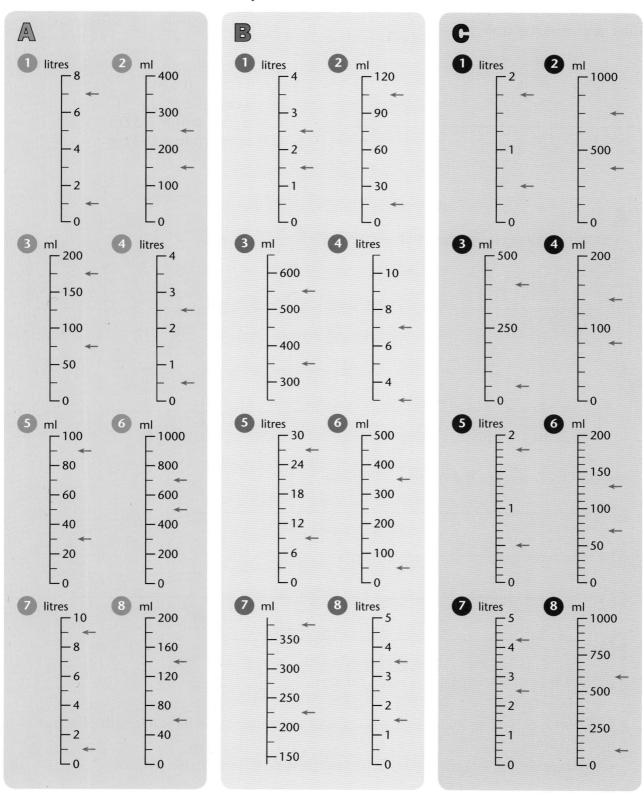

TARGET   To measure and draw straight lines in cm and mm.

Start measuring from 0,
not from the end of the
ruler, and read the scale.

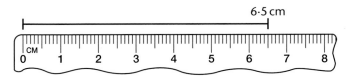

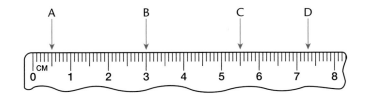

A = 5 mm = 0·5 cm
B = 3 cm
C = 5 cm 5 mm = 5·5 cm
D = 7 cm 3 mm = 7·3 cm

A

Read the measurements shown on each ruler.

1

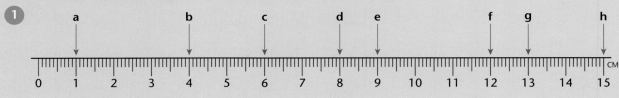

2

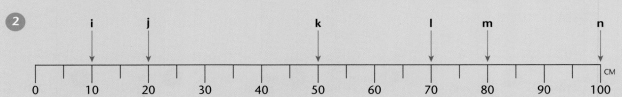

Measure these lines to the nearest centimetre.

3 |———————————————————|

4 |—————————————|

5 |————————————————————————|

6 |———————————————|

7 Draw lines of 12 cm, 5 cm, 13 cm and 8 cm.

8 **a)** Write down five things in the classroom which you think have a length of about
      15 cm.

   b) Measure the length of each object to the nearest centimetre.

B

Read the measurements shown on each ruler.

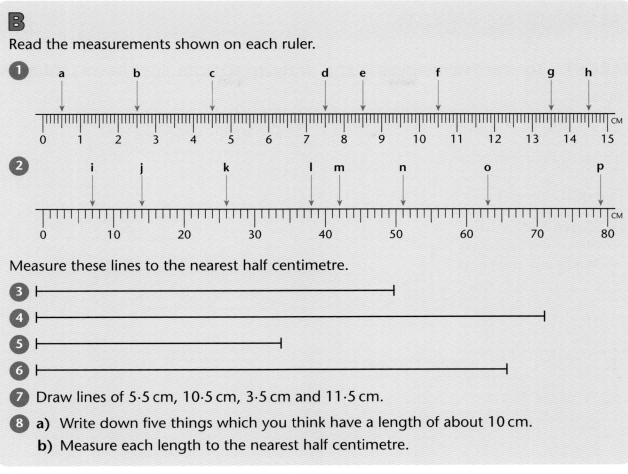

1

2

Measure these lines to the nearest half centimetre.

3

4

5

6

7 Draw lines of 5·5 cm, 10·5 cm, 3·5 cm and 11·5 cm.

8 a) Write down five things which you think have a length of about 10 cm.

b) Measure each length to the nearest half centimetre.

C

1 Read the measurements shown to the nearest millimetre.

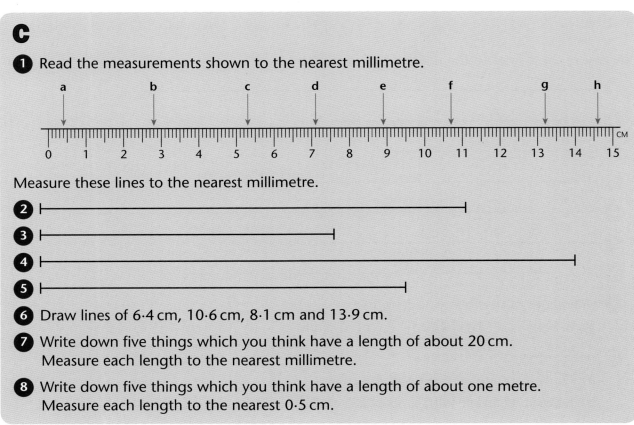

Measure these lines to the nearest millimetre.

2

3

4

5

6 Draw lines of 6·4 cm, 10·6 cm, 8·1 cm and 13·9 cm.

7 Write down five things which you think have a length of about 20 cm.
Measure each length to the nearest millimetre.

8 Write down five things which you think have a length of about one metre.
Measure each length to the nearest 0·5 cm.

TARGET   To practise measuring and drawing straight lines in cm and mm.

Examples

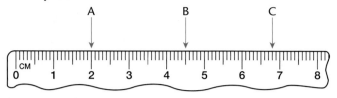

A = 2 cm
B = 4 cm 5 mm = 4·5 cm
C = 6 cm 8 mm = 6·8 cm

D = 25 mm = 2 cm 5 mm
E = 49 mm = 4 cm 9 mm
F = 74 mm = 7 cm 4 mm

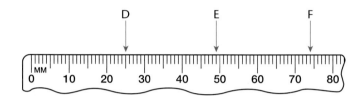

A

1   Read the measurements shown on the ruler.

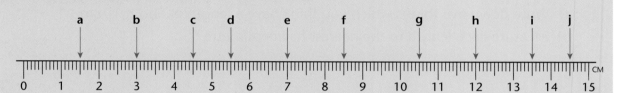

Measure these lines to the nearest half centimetre.

2 ├──┤

3 ├──────────────────────────────┤

4 ├────────────────────┤

5 ├──────────────────────────────┤

6 ├──┤

7 ├──────────────────────┤

8 ├──────────────────────────────────┤

9   Draw lines of the following lengths.

     a) 8·5 cm   **b)** 12 cm   **c)** 5·5 cm   **d)** 13·5 cm   **e)** 10·5 cm

10   Use a set square and ruler.

     a) Draw a square with sides of 4·5 cm.

     b) Draw a rectangle with sides of 2·5 cm and 6·5 cm.

B

1 Read the measurements shown on the ruler.

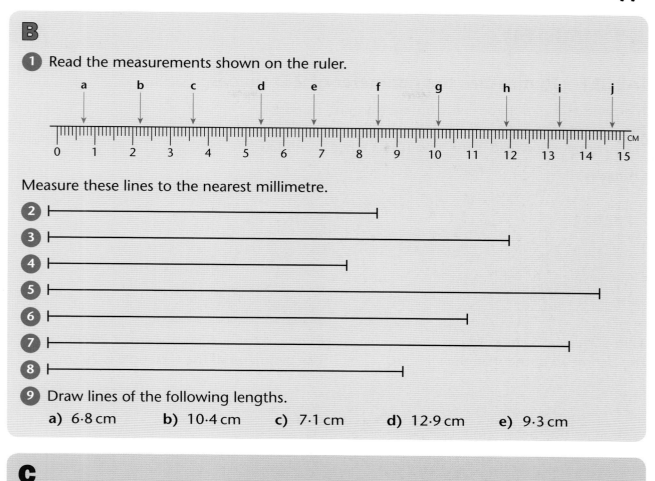

Measure these lines to the nearest millimetre.

2 ├──┤

3 ├──┤

4 ├──────────────────────────────┤

5 ├──┤

6 ├──────────────────────────────────────┤

7 ├──┤

8 ├─────────────────────────────────┤

9 Draw lines of the following lengths.

　　a) 6·8 cm　　　　**b)** 10·4 cm　　　**c)** 7·1 cm　　　**d)** 12·9 cm　　　**e)** 9·3 cm

C

1 For each shape:

　　a) measure the sides

　　b) find the total length around the shape (the perimeter) by adding the lengths of
　　　the sides together.

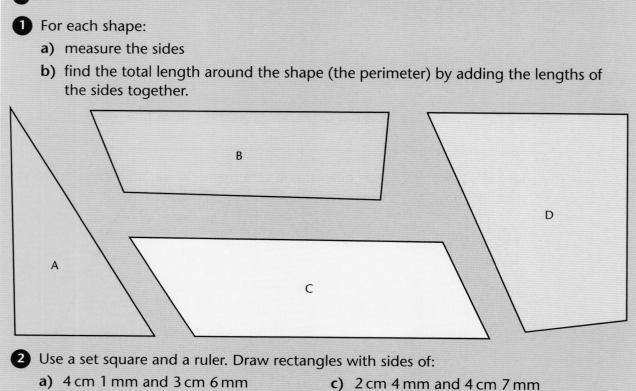

2 Use a set square and a ruler. Draw rectangles with sides of:

　　a) 4 cm 1 mm and 3 cm 6 mm　　　　　**c)** 2 cm 4 mm and 4 cm 7 mm

　　b) 5 cm 8 mm and 2 cm 3 mm　　　　　**d)** 3 cm 9 mm and 6 cm 2 mm.

TARGET   To measure the perimeter of 2-D shapes.

The perimeter of a shape is the distance around its edges.
The perimeter of a room is the total length of its walls.
The perimeter of a field is the length of a fence around it.

Examples

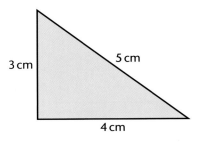

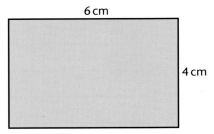

3 cm + 4 cm + 5 cm = 12 cm
The perimeter of the triangle is 12 cm.

6 cm + 4 cm + 6 cm + 4 cm = 20 cm
The perimeter of the rectangle is 20 cm.

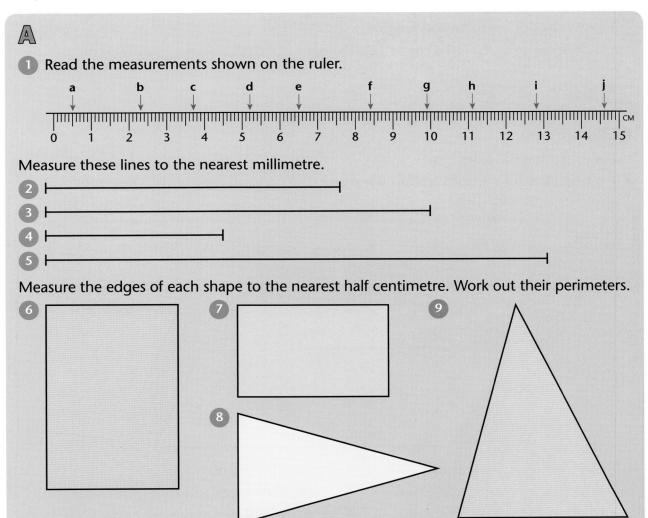

A

1 Read the measurements shown on the ruler.

Measure these lines to the nearest millimetre.

2

3

4

5

Measure the edges of each shape to the nearest half centimetre. Work out their perimeters.

6

7

9

8

B

Measure the edges of each shape to the nearest millimetre. Work out the perimeters.

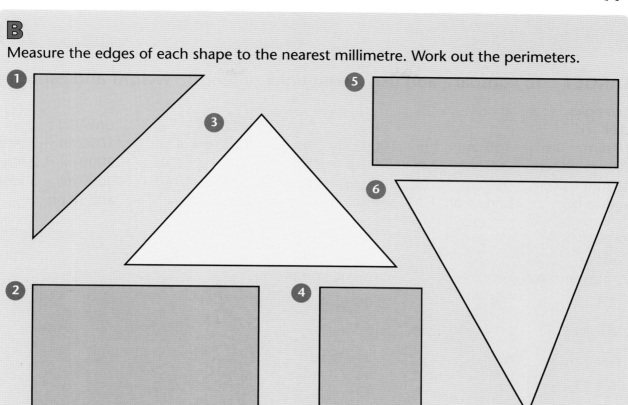

C

Use squared paper.

1. Draw three different rectangles, each with a perimeter of 14 cm.

2. Draw the following rectangles and work out their perimeters.
   a) 4 cm by 2 cm 6 mm
   b) 5 cm by 3 cm 9 mm.

3. Copy and complete this table showing measurements of rectangles.

Length (cm)	4	2	3	5			2		4	
Width (cm)	5	8			12	7		8		12
Perimeter (cm)	18		18	50	36	42	18	40	28	120

Work out the perimeter of each of the rooms shown in these floor plans.
All the lengths are in metres.

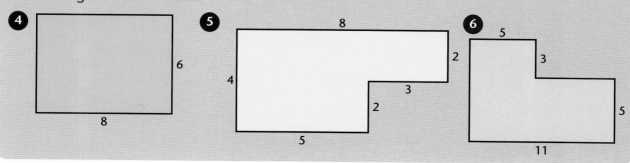

TARGET To compare and use mixed units of length, weight and capacity.

Examples

LENGTH

			WEIGHT	CAPACITY
10 mm = 1 cm	100 cm = 1 m	1000 m = 1 km	1000 g = 1 kg	1000 ml = 1 litre
20 mm = 2 cm	200 cm = 2 m	2000 m = 2 km	2000 g = 2 kg	2000 ml = 2 litres
30 mm = 3 cm	300 cm = 3 m	3000 m = 3 km	3000 g = 3 kg	3000 ml = 3 litres
and so on	and so on	and so on	and so on	and so on

A
Copy and complete.

1. 1 litre = ☐ ml
2. 2 kg = ☐ g
3. 1 m = ☐ cm
4. 1 km = ☐ m

5. 2 cm = ☐ mm
6. 3 m = ☐ cm
7. 1 kg = ☐ g
8. 2 km = ☐ m

9. 5 cm = ☐ mm
10. 2 m = ☐ cm
11. 4 km = ☐ m
12. 3 litres = ☐ ml

13. 5 kg = ☐ g
14. 3 cm = ☐ mm
15. 4 litres = ☐ ml
16. 5 m = ☐ cm

17. 4 km = ☐ m
18. 1 cm = ☐ mm
19. 3 kg = ☐ g
20. 2 litres = ☐ ml

B
Copy and complete.

1. 9000 m = ☐ km
2. 5 litres = ☐ ml
3. 700 cm = ☐ m
4. $\frac{1}{2}$ kg = ☐ g

5. 100 mm = ☐ cm
6. 6 m = ☐ cm
7. $\frac{1}{2}$ km = ☐ m
8. 8000 g = ☐ kg

9. 8 cm = ☐ mm
10. $\frac{1}{2}$ litre = ☐ ml
11. 50 cm = ☐ m
12. 4 kg = ☐ g

13. 5 km = ☐ m
14. 4000 ml = ☐ litres
15. $\frac{1}{2}$ cm = ☐ mm
16. 10 000 g = ☐ kg

17. 7 litres = ☐ ml
18. 600 mm = ☐ cm
19. 6 km = ☐ m
20. 1000 cm = ☐ m

C
Copy and complete.

1. 650 ml + ☐ = I litre
2. 450 g + ☐ = I kg
3. 75 cm + ☐ = I m
4. 250 m + ☐ = I km

5. 50 g + ☐ = I kg
6. 350 ml + ☐ = I litre
7. 95 cm + ☐ = I m
8. 550 m + ☐ = I km

9. 150 g + ☐ = I kg
10. 45 cm + ☐ = I m
11. 50 m + ☐ = I km
12. 750 ml + ☐ = I litre

13. 850 g + ☐ = 1 kg
14. 350 m + ☐ = 1 km
15. 65 cm + ☐ = 1 m
16. 950 ml + ☐ = 1 litre

17. 750 m + ☐ = 1 km
18. 550 g + ☐ = 1 kg
19. 250 ml + ☐ = 1 litre
20. 15 cm + ☐ = 1 m

TARGET To use and compare mixed units of length, weight and capacity.

Examples

LENGTH
25 mm = 2 cm 5 mm
190 cm = 1 m 90 cm
6300 m = 6 km 300 m

WEIGHT
3000 g = 3 kg 0 g
270 g = 0 kg 270 g
1200 g = 1 kg 200 g

CAPACITY
6000 ml = 6 ℓ (litres)
3250 ml = 3 ℓ 250 ml
2400 ml = 2 ℓ 400 ml

A

Copy and complete.

1. 1 kg = ☐ g
2. 2 m = ☐ cm
3. 7 km = ☐ m
4. 3 litres = ☐ ml
5. 10 mm = ☐ cm
6. 3000 m = ☐ km
7. 2000 g = ☐ kg
8. 100 cm = ☐ m
9. 1 litre = ☐ ml
10. 5 cm = ☐ mm
11. 2 km = ☐ m
12. 9 m = ☐ cm
13. 80 mm = ☐ cm
14. 5000 g = ☐ kg
15. 2000 ml = ☐ litres
16. 1000 m = ☐ km
17. 3 m = ☐ cm
18. 2 cm = ☐ mm
19. 6 kg = ☐ g
20. 7 litres = ☐ ml

B

Copy and complete.

1. 1 km 300 m = ☐ m
2. 5 m 60 cm = ☐ cm
3. 7 litres 900 ml = ☐ ml
4. 1 cm 2 mm = ☐ mm
5. 3500 g = ☐ kg ☐ g
6. 190 cm = ☐ m ☐ cm
7. 6200 m = ☐ km ☐ m
8. 73 mm = ☐ cm ☐ mm
9. 1 litre 400 ml = ☐ ml
10. 6 cm 5 mm = ☐ mm
11. 2 km 700 m = ☐ m
12. 5 kg 100 g = ☐ g
13. 980 cm = ☐ m ☐ cm
14. 4300 ml = ☐ litres ☐ ml
15. 38 mm = ☐ cm ☐ mm
16. 8400 g = ☐ kg ☐ g
17. 2 litres 600 ml = ☐ ml
18. 4 m 10 cm = ☐ cm
19. 8 km 500 m = ☐ m
20. 1 kg 700 g = ☐ g

C

Copy and complete.

1. 370 m + ☐ = 1 km
2. 63 cm + ☐ = 1 m
3. 150 ml + ☐ = 1 litre
4. 910 g + ☐ = 1 kg
5. 440 mm + ☐ = 1 m
6. 890 ml + ☐ = 1 litre
7. 22 cm + ☐ = 1 m
8. 580 g + ☐ = 1 kg
9. 760 m + ☐ = 1 km
10. 20 ml + ☐ = 1 litre
11. 84 cm + ☐ = 1 m
12. 350 g + ☐ = 1 kg
13. 280 mm + ☐ = 1 m
14. 99 cm + ☐ = 1 m
15. 740 g + ☐ = 1 kg
16. 660 ml + ☐ = 1 litre
17. 35 cm + ☐ = 1 m
18. 430 ml + ☐ = 1 litre
19. 170 g + ☐ = 1 kg
20. 590 m + ☐ = 1 km

TARGET To use mental methods to add and subtract pairs of one- and two-digit numbers involving measures.

A
Write the answer only.

1. 8p + 6p
2. £9 + £8
3. 25p + 9p
4. £76 + £7
5. 24p + 20p
6. £39 + £50

7. 15 g − 7 g
8. 13 kg − 4 kg
9. 51 g − 5 g
10. 94 kg − 9 kg
11. 75 g − 30 g
12. 58 kg − 20 kg

13. 7 cm + 5 cm
14. 6 m + 9 m
15. 39 cm + 3 cm
16. 64 m + 8 m
17. 47 cm + 30 cm
18. 52 m + 40 m

19. 18 ml − 9 ml
20. 14 litres − 7 litres
21. 35 ml − 8 ml
22. 80 litres − 6 litres
23. 83 ml − 20 ml
24. 95 litres − 60 litres

B
Write the answer only.

1. 80 g + 50 g
2. 90 g + 60 g
3. 42 m + 80 m
4. 75 m + 90 m

5. 23 ℓ + 27 ℓ (litres)
6. 37 ℓ + 58 ℓ
7. £59 + £25
8. £36 + £37

9. 90 ml + 50 ml
10. 80 ml + 90 ml
11. 77 kg + 60 kg
12. 94 kg + 20 kg

13. 38p + 44p
14. 45p + 26p
15. 24 cm + 39 cm
16. 69 cm + 28 cm

17. 140 g − 60 g
18. 170 g − 80 g
19. 119 m − 50 m
20. 153 m − 70 m

21. 72 ℓ − 25 ℓ
22. 55 ℓ − 19 ℓ
23. £90 − £45
24. £84 − £56

25. 160 ml − 80 ml
26. 120 ml − 50 ml
27. 186 kg − 90 kg
28. 114 kg − 30 kg

29. 61p − 34p
30. 73p − 18p
31. 96 cm − 57 cm
32. 82 cm − 39 cm

C
Copy and complete.

1. 60 ml + ☐ = 120 ml
2. 90 ml + ☐ = 160 ml
3. £85 + ☐ = £145
4. £31 + ☐ = £111
5. 56 kg + ☐ = 141 kg
6. 94 kg + ☐ = 163 kg
7. 48 m + ☐ = 122 m
8. 89 m + ☐ = 135 m
9. 140 g − ☐ = 70 g
10. 130 g − ☐ = 90 g
11. 173 ℓ − ☐ = 83 ℓ (litres)
12. 159 ℓ − ☐ = 79 ℓ
13. ☐ − 75 km = 59 km
14. ☐ − 54 km = 67 km
15. ☐ − £68 = £78
16. ☐ − £97 = £55

TARGET To use mental methods to add and subtract 1s, 10s or 100s to 3-digit numbers involving measures.

A

Write the answer only.

1. 36 cm + 7 cm
2. 25 cm + 50 cm
3. 63 m + 100 m
4. 94 m − 8 m
5. 48 cm − 20 cm
6. 770 m − 100 m
7. 83 g + 8 g
8. 68 kg + 30 kg
9. 740 g + 100 g
10. 27 kg − 9 kg
11. 95 g − 40 g
12. 410 kg − 100 kg
13. 59 ℓ + 6 ℓ (litres)
14. 32 ml + 20 ml
15. 240 ml + 100 ml
16. 83 ℓ − 5 ℓ
17. 74 ml − 30 ml
18. 960 ml − 100 ml
19. £24 + £9
20. 45 p + 40 p
21. £890 + £100
22. 51 p − 7p
23. 82 p − 60 p
24. £530 − £100

B

Write the answer only.

1. 518 m + 7 m
2. 173 ml + 50 ml
3. 436 g + 200 g
4. £851 − £8
5. 685 m − 300 m
6. 222 g − 40 g
7. 754 m + 60 m
8. £367 + £400
9. 199 ℓ + 4 ℓ (litres)
10. 745 ml − 500 ml
11. £932 − £90
12. 484 kg − 6 kg
13. 563 m + 300 m
14. £828 + £9
15. 397 g + 70 g
16. 363 ml − 80 ml
17. 847 g − 400 g
18. 596 m − 9 m
19. 159 kg + 3 kg
20. 412 ml + 500 ml
21. £668 + £80
22. 285 ℓ − 7 ℓ
23. 914 m − 60 m
24. £639 − £200
25. 343 ml + 70 ml
26. 796 m + 9 m
27. 207 kg + 600 kg
28. 528 g − 70 g
29. 976 ml − 600 ml
30. £841 − £5

C

Copy and complete.

1. ☐ + 30 g = 604 g
2. ☐ + 8 ℓ = 323 ℓ (litres)
3. ☐ + 600 ml = 1389 ml
4. ☐ − 9 kg = 233 kg
5. ☐ − 70 m = 891 m
6. ☐ − £200 = £106
7. ☐ + 9 m = 902 m
8. ☐ + 300 g = 828 g
9. ☐ + £50 = £545
10. ☐ − 80 ml = 59 ml
11. ☐ − 400 m = 227 m
12. ☐ − £6 = £899
13. ☐ + 800 g = 1232 g
14. ☐ + 70 m = 323 m
15. ☐ + 6 kg = 594 kg

TARGET   To count measures in 1s, 10s, and 100s from a given quantity.

Examples

Count on £50 from £689

+£10 +£10 +£10 +£10 +£10

£689   £699   £709   £719   £729   £739

Count on 400 m from 375 m

+100m +100m +100m +100m

375m   475m   575m   675m   775m

A

Count on

1 6 p from 36 p

2 9 p from 54 p

3 4 p from 27 p

4 7 cm from 83 cm

5 5 cm from 49 cm

6 8 cm from 65 cm

7 20 mm from 50 mm

8 50 mm from 40 mm

9 30 mm from 35 mm

10 70 g from 25 g

11 40 g from 40 g

12 60 g from 15 g

Write the next four measures in each sequence.

13 £56, £57, £58

14 £25, £26, £27

15 £77, £78, £79

16 20 m, 30 m, 40 m

17 5 m, 15 m, 25 m

18 32 m, 42 m, 52 m

B

Count on

1 7 litres from 312 litres

2 9 litres from 645 litres

3 6 litres from 287 litres

4 8 litres from 523 litres

5 40 g from 875 g

6 70 g from 150 g

7 50 g from 490 g

8 90 g from 385 g

9 300 m from 160 m

10 600 m from 230 m

11 500 m from 415 m

12 400 m from 341 m

Write the next five measures in each sequence.

13 733 km, 734 km, 735 km

14 396 km, 397 km, 398 km

15 £553, £563, £573

16 £138, £148, £158

17 280 ml, 380 ml, 480 ml

18 45 ml, 145 ml, 245 ml

C

Count on

1 8 km from 3615 km

2 5 km from 1286 km

3 9 km from 9073 km

4 7 km from 2457 km

5 £60 from £4346

6 £80 from £6193

7 £40 from £1587

8 £90 from £7961

9 500 ml from 8750 ml

10 700 ml from 1480 ml

11 900 ml from 7190 ml

12 600 ml from 2965 ml

Write the next five measures in each sequence.

13 9185 m, 9186 m, 9187 m

14 2423 m, 2424 m, 2425 m

15 1975 kg, 1985 kg, 1995 kg

16 7239 kg, 7249 kg, 7259 kg

17 £3640, £3740, £3840

18 £5418, £5528, £5638

TARGET   To add or subtract lengths using written methods.

Examples

```
    m   cm
    4   28
 +  3   17
 ─────────
    7   45
          1
```

```
    cm  mm
   7 13  1
    8  4  3
 -  5  9  5
 ──────────
    2  4  8
```

A

Copy and complete.

1
```
    cm
    53
 +  45
```

2
```
    cm
    36
 +  21
```

3
```
    cm
    45
 +  34
```

4
```
    m
    61
 +  19
```

5
```
    m
    54
 +  37
```

6
```
    m
    45
 +  26
```

7
```
    cm
    45
 -  33
```

8
```
    cm
    79
 -  52
```

9
```
    cm
    57
 -  44
```

10
```
    m
    81
 -  16
```

11
```
    m
    63
 -  25
```

12
```
    m
    94
 -  77
```

13 A playground is 34 m wide. Its length is 19 m more than its width. How long is the playground?

14 A strip of paper is 82 cm long. 25 cm is cut off. How long is the strip which is left?

B

Copy and complete.

1
```
     m
    185
 +   73
```

2
```
     m
    436
 +  144
```

3
```
    m  cm
    5  92
 +  2  57
```

4
```
    m  cm
    3  47
 +  3  29
```

5
```
    cm  mm
    75   0
 +  16   5
```

6
```
    cm  mm
    41   4
 +  29   8
```

7
```
     m
    173
 -  126
```

8
```
     m
    618
 -  332
```

9
```
    m  cm
    8  64
 -  4  59
```

10
```
    m  cm
    4  05
 -  2  37
```

11
```
    cm  mm
    73   1
 -  39   5
```

12
```
    cm  mm
    54   2
 -  26   8
```

13 A rock face is 240 m high. Lesley has climbed 127 m. How far does she still have to climb to reach the top?

C

Copy and complete.

1
```
    m  cm
    38 49
 +   2 43
```

2
```
    40m 92cm
    m  cm
    27 15
 + 12 57
```

3
```
    2972
     1 1
    m  cm
    44 63
 + 25 72
```

4
```
    7035
     1 1
    m  cm
    53 98
 + 41 86
```

5
```
    9584
     1 1
    m  cm
    36 72
 + 28 64
```

6
```
    6536
     1 1 1
    m  cm
    49 56
 + 30 45
    80 01
```

7
```
    m  cm
    26 51
 - 13 47
```

8
```
    m  cm
    37 25
 - 35 28
```

9
```
    m  cm
    64 08
 - 18 16
```

10
```
    m  cm
    93 92
 - 57 55
```

11
```
    m  cm
    46 53
 - 19 64
```

12
```
    m  cm
    80 47
 -  8 59
```

13 A tree is 13 m 84 cm tall. The top of a block of flats is 28 m 36 cm higher than the top of the tree. How tall is the block of flats?

14 A corridor is 52 m 30 cm long. 29 m 64 cm of its length has been painted. How long is the corridor which has not been painted?

TARGET   To add or subtract weights using written methods.

Examples

```
      g
    5 8 7
  + 3 2 6
  ───────
    9 1 3
    ¹ ¹
```

```
    kg   g
   4  1  6  1
   5̸  1  7̸ 0
  - 2  8  5  6
  ───────────
    2  3  1  4
```

A

Copy and complete.

1
```
      g
     34
   + 26
```

2
```
      g
     43
   + 18
```

3
```
      g
     67
   + 25
```

4
```
     kg
     52
   + 44
```

5
```
     kg
     39
   + 35
```

6
```
     kg
     46
   + 17
```

7
```
      g
     36
   - 23
```

8
```
      g
     84
   - 32
```

9
```
      g
     58
   - 18
```

10
```
     kg
     72
   - 44
```

11
```
     kg
     95
   - 39
```

12
```
     kg
     60
   - 16
```

13 Ida has two suitcases. One weighs 35 kg and the other weighs 18 kg. What is the weight of the two suitcases together?

14 A salt pot holds 80 g. 55 g is used. How much is left?

B

Copy and complete.

1
```
      g
    248
  + 123
```

2
```
      g
    653
  + 186
```

3
```
      g
    327
  + 158
```

4
```
    kg   g
    5 950
  + 2 420
```

5
```
    kg   g
    4 060
  + 1 580
```

6
```
    kg   g
    3 740
  + 2 390
```

7
```
      g
    450
  - 127
```

8
```
      g
    729
  - 263
```

9
```
      g
    574
  - 335
```

10
```
    kg   g
    9 410
  -   780
```

11
```
    kg   g
    6 060
  - 2 480
```

12
```
    kg   g
    8 320
  - 5 590
```

13 The lighter of two parcels weighs 2 kg 670 g. The other parcel weighs 1 kg 560 g more. What is the weight of the heavier parcel?

14 A bag holds 6 kg 500 g of potatoes. 3 kg 720 g is used. How much is left?

C

Copy and complete.

1
```
    kg   g
    1 485
  +   357
```

2
```
    kg   g
    3 729
  +   648
```

3
```
    kg   g
    5 066
  + 1 259
```

4
```
    kg   g
    6 394
  + 2 725
```

5
```
    kg   g
    4 853
  + 3 794
```

6
```
    kg   g
    2 617
  + 1 874
```

7
```
    kg   g
    3 163
  -   728
```

8
```
    kg   g
    4 049
  - 2 392
```

9
```
    kg   g
    8 183
  - 4 654
```

10
```
    kg   g
    6 327
  -   937
```

11
```
    kg   g
    7 531
  - 3 475
```

12
```
    kg   g
    9 248
  -   562
```

13 Bobby weighs 8 kg 140 g. Buster weighs 3 kg 457 g. How much heavier is Bobby than Buster?

TARGET   To add or subtract capacities using written methods.

Examples

```
   ℓ  ml                    ml
   3 694                 6  14 1
 + 2 178                  7 5 0
 ───────               − 1 6 3
   5 872                 ─────────
     1 1                   5 8 7
```

A

Copy and complete.

1
```
      ml
      26
   + 16
```

2
```
      ml
      51
   + 44
```

3
```
      ml
      33
   + 37
```

4
```
    litres
      47
   + 25
```

5
```
    litres
      62
   + 19
```

6
```
    litres
      55
   + 38
```

7
```
      ml
      55
   − 24
```

8
```
      ml
      78
   − 33
```

9
```
      ml
      36
   − 19
```

10
```
       ℓ
      64
   − 52
```

11
```
       ℓ
      91
   − 27
```

12
```
       ℓ
      85
   − 68
```

13 An artist mixes 65 ml of yellow paint and 29 ml of red paint. How much orange paint has she made?

B

Copy and complete.

1
```
      ml
     390
   + 53
```

2
```
      ml
     534
   +174
```

3
```
      ml
     262
   +257
```

4
```
    ℓ  ml
   4 180
 + 3 450
```

5
```
    ℓ  ml
   6 560
 + 1 790
```

6
```
    ℓ  ml
   4 870
 + 1 460
```

7
```
      ml
     362
   − 235
```

8
```
      ml
     859
   − 476
```

9
```
      ml
     480
   − 154
```

10
```
    ℓ  ml
   9 170
 − 8 350
```

11
```
    ℓ  ml
   7 430
 − 3 960
```

12
```
    ℓ  ml
   5 680
 − 3 520
```

13 A small bucket has a capacity of 3 litres 750 ml. A larger bucket has 1 litre 385 ml more capacity. What is the capacity of the larger bucket?

14 A bottle of cooking oil holds 725 ml. 350 ml is used. How much is left?

C

Copy and complete.

1
```
    ℓ  ml
   2 682
 + 1 385
```

2
```
    ℓ  ml
   5 437
 +   654
```

3
```
    ℓ  ml
   1 945
 + 1 383
```

4
```
    ℓ  ml
   4 218
 + 2 867
```

5
```
    ℓ  ml
   5 683
 + 3 726
```

6
```
    ℓ  ml
   6 579
 + 1 908
```

7
```
    ℓ  ml
   4 237
 −   783
```

8
```
    ℓ  ml
   2 160
 − 1 829
```

9
```
    ℓ  ml
   6 954
 − 2 467
```

10
```
    ℓ  ml
   8 306
 − 5 390
```

11
```
    ℓ  ml
   7 521
 − 6 984
```

12
```
    ℓ  ml
   9 042
 −   735
```

13 One can of paint holds 4 litres 985 ml. A second can holds 2 litres 635 ml. How much paint is there altogether?

14 A large watering can holds 8 litres 430 ml. A smaller can holds 5 litres 675 ml. What is the difference in the capacity of the cans?

TARGET   To read the time displayed on analogue or digital clocks to the nearest minute using am and pm.

Examples

Analogue clocks have faces.
Read the minutes as:
'past' before 30 minutes
'to' after 30 minutes.

morning   afternoon

am means before 12 noon
pm means after 12 noon

27 minutes past 7   18 minutes to 5
7:27 am   4:42 pm

Digital clocks have figures only.
The minutes are always shown as
minutes past the hour.

A

Write the time shown on each of these clocks in words.

1   6:40   **3**   9:50   **5**   5:30   **7**   1:35   **9**   4:55

2   3:25   **4**   12:15   **6**   11:05   **8**   8:20   **10**   10:45

Write the time shown on each of these clocks in words and figures.

11   **13**   **15**   **17**   **19**

12   **14**   **16**   **18**   **20**

21   Write these times in figures: **a)** half past eight   **c)** eleven o'clock
                                       b) quarter to three   **d)** quarter past six

B

Write the time shown on each of these clocks to the nearest minute:

a) in words **b)** in figures using am and pm.

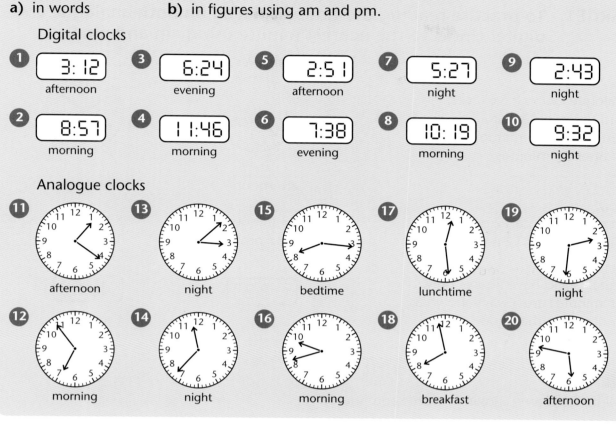

Digital clocks

1 `3:12` afternoon   3 `6:24` evening   5 `2:51` afternoon   7 `5:27` night   9 `2:43` night

2 `8:57` morning   4 `11:46` morning   6 `7:38` evening   8 `10:19` morning   10 `9:32` night

Analogue clocks

11 afternoon   13 night   15 bedtime   17 lunchtime   19 night

12 morning   14 night   16 morning   18 breakfast   20 afternoon

C

24-hour clocks always have four digits on display. Midnight is 00:00.

Examples 8:22 pm is 20:22
6:48 am is 06:48

1 Copy and complete the table.

TIME IN WORDS	12-HOUR CLOCK	24-HOUR CLOCK
12 minutes to 5 in the morning	4:48 am	04:48
28 minutes to 2 in the afternoon		
		18:06
	11:21 am	
14 minutes past midnight		
	10:49 pm	
		05:05
23 minutes past 4 in the afternoon		
	8:09 am	
		15:54
	9:17 pm	
7 minutes to 2 at night		

TARGET   To practise reading the time displayed on both analogue and digital clocks to the nearest minute using am and pm.

Examples

Analogue clocks have faces.
Read the minutes as:
'past' before 30 minutes
'to' after 30 minutes.

am means before 12 noon
pm means after 12 noon

Digital clocks have figures only.
The minutes are always shown as minutes past the hour.

afternoon

23 minutes to 4
3:37 pm

3:37

morning

8 minutes past 10
10:08 am

10:08

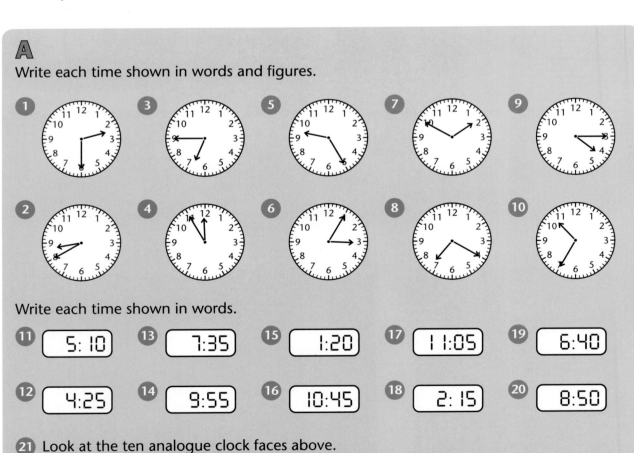

A
Write each time shown in words and figures.

1   3   5   7   9

2   4   6   8   10

Write each time shown in words.

11   5:10   13   7:35   15   1:20   17   11:05   19   6:40

12   4:25   14   9:55   16   10:45   18   2:15   20   8:50

21 Look at the ten analogue clock faces above.
    Write the times in figures half an hour after the times shown.
    Example   1 3:00

B

Write each time shown to the nearest minute:
a) in words   b) in figures using am or pm.

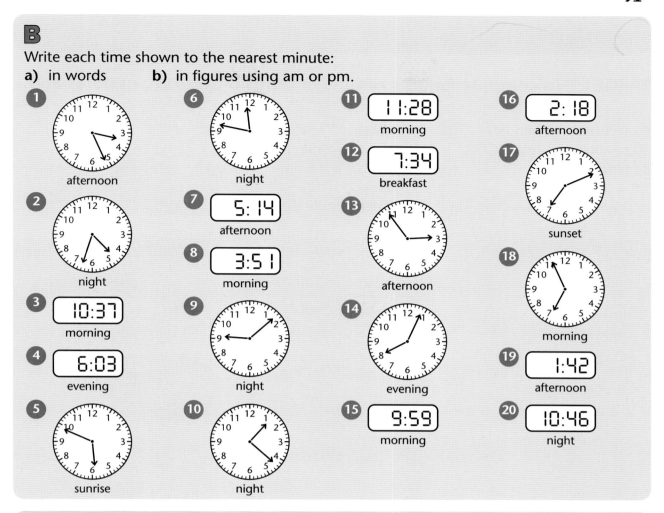

1 afternoon

2 night

3 10:37 morning

4 6:03 evening

5 sunrise

6 night

7 5:14 afternoon

8 3:51 morning

9 night

10 night

11 11:28 morning

12 7:34 breakfast

13 afternoon

14 evening

15 9:59 morning

16 2:18 afternoon

17 sunset

18 morning

19 1:42 afternoon

20 10:46 night

C

24-hour clocks always have four digits on display. Midnight is 00:00.

Examples   8:22 pm is 20:22
6:48 am is 06:48

Copy and complete the table.

TIME IN WORDS	12-HOUR CLOCK	24-HOUR CLOCK
27 minutes past 4 in the afternoon	4:27 pm	16:27
	7:36 am	
	10:53 pm	
		09:48
		13:02
	8:21 pm	
	5:38 am	
		23:57
		06:13
	4:52 am	
	2:49 pm	
		10:29

TARGET To compare lengths of time in terms of seconds, minutes and hours.

60 seconds = 1 minute
60 minutes = 1 hour
24 hours = 1 day

Example
How many minutes are left in the hour if the time is 3:10?
Answer
50 minutes are left. (60 − 10 = 50)

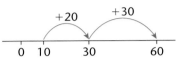

A

How many seconds make:

1. 1 minute
2. 2 minutes
3. half a minute
4. one and a half minutes?

How many minutes make:

5. one hour
6. a quarter of an hour
7. half an hour
8. three quarters of an hour?

How many minutes are left in the hour if the time is:

9. half past
10. quarter to
11. quarter past
12. 10 past?

How many hours make:

13. 1 day
14. half a day
15. two days
16. a quarter of a day?

B

How many seconds make:

1. one and a half minutes
2. a quarter of a minute
3. one and a quarter minutes
4. two and a half minutes?

How many minutes make:

5. two hours
6. one and a half hours
7. two and a quarter hours
8. one and three quarter hours?

How many minutes are left in the hour if the time is:

9. 2:20
10. 6:50
11. 1:10
12. 11:35
13. 8:05
14. 3:40
15. 10:25
16. 5:55?

How many hours are left in the day if the time is:

17. 6:00 in the evening
18. 9:00 in the morning
19. 11:00 at night
20. 2:00 in the afternoon?

C

How many minutes are:

1. 600 seconds
2. 180 seconds
3. 240 seconds
4. 450 seconds?

How many hours are:

5. 300 minutes
6. 420 minutes
7. 210 minutes
8. 195 minutes?

How many minutes are left in the hour if the time is:

9. 9:38
10. 4:13
11. 2:52
12. 7:26
13. 10:41
14. 5:07
15. 8:34
16. 3:19?

How many hours and minutes are left in the day if the time is:

17. 8:27 in the evening
18. 7:14 in the morning
19. 1:32 in the afternoon
20. 10:58 in the morning?

TARGET   To know the number of days in each month, year and leap year.

30 days has September,
April, June and November.
All the rest have 31,
Save for February alone,
Which has but 28 days clear
And 29 in each leap year.

There are 365 days in each year and 366 in each leap year.

Leap years occur every four years. The years which are leap years are easy to remember because they are multiples of four.

2004, 2008, 2012, 2016, etc.

A

How many days are in:

1. July
2. November
3. February next year
4. April and May altogether?

DECEMBER						
Sun	M	Tu	W	Th	F	Sa
			1	2	3	4
5	6	7	8	9	10	11
12	13	14	15	16	17	18
19	20	21	22	23	24	25
26	27	28	29	30	31	

Look at the calendar. On what day of the week will these dates fall?

5. Christmas Day
6. New Year's Eve
7. St. Andrew's Day November 30th
8. Start of new term January 5th
9. What is the date one week before:
   a) April 22nd
   b) August 3rd?
10. What is the date one week after:
    a) January 16th
    b) June 27th?

B

1. What will be the date two weeks after:
   a) July 19th
   b) May 24?
2. What will be the date two weeks before:
   a) May 8th
   b) November 13th?

SEPTEMBER 2018						
Sun	M	Tu	W	Th	F	Sa
					1	2
3	4	5	6	7	8	9
10	11	12	13	14	15	16
17	18	19	20	21	22	23
24	25	26	27	28	29	30

Use the above calendar. On what day of the week do these birthdays fall?

3. Jan – September 14th
4. Phil – September 26th
5. Alan – October 6th
6. Sheila – August 28th
7. Write out the calendar for August 2018.
8. How many days are there in a leap year?
9. How many days are there in a year which is not a leap year?

C

1. What will be the date four weeks after:
   a) February 9th 2018
   b) April 21st?
2. What will be the date three weeks before:
   a) August 4th
   b) December 15th?
3. How often is there a leap year?
4. When is the next leap year?
5. Which of these years is a leap year?
   a) 2024   c) 2034
   b) 2066   d) 2076
6. In 2020 St David's Day, March 1st, will fall on a Sunday. On which day will the following dates fall?
   a) St Patrick's Day March 17th
   b) St George's Day April 23rd
   c) St Valentine's Day February 14th
   d) Burn's Night (Scotland) January 25th

TARGET To use information presented in tables to calculate lengths of time.

BBC1		ITV1	
2:10	Coast	2:05	Fortune (Quiz)
2:25	Rugby (Sport)	2:45	Oliver Twist (Film)
4:25	Mastermind (Quiz)	4:50	The Rescuers (Drama)
4:55	National News	5:45	Local News
5:20	Local News	6:05	National News
5:30	Merlin (Drama)	6:20	TV Fun (Comedy)
6:35	Come Dancing	6:55	X Factor On Ice
8:25	Casualty (Drama)	8:10	Law and Order (Drama)
9:15	Comedy Live (Comedy)	9:05	X Factor Results
10:00	National News	9:50	National News
10:20	Football (Sport)	10:10	Celebrity Chat
11:45	Sky At Night	11:40	The Zone

A

Which programme starts at:

1. 9:15
2. 2:05
3. 11:40
4. 2:25
5. 5:30
6. 6:55
7. 4:55
8. 5:45?

How long is:

9. Coast
10. TV Fun
11. Mastermind
12. X Factor Results?

Which programme can you watch:

13. on BBC 1 at 6:00
14. on ITV 1 at 7:00
15. on BBC 1 at 3:00
16. on ITV 1 at 9:00
17. on BBC 1 at 8:00
18. on ITV 1 at 5:00

B

Which programme finishes at:

1. 11:40
2. 5:30
3. 2:45
4. 4:25
5. 9:05
6. 11:45
7. 6:05
8. 8:25

How long is:

9. Casualty
10. The Rescuers
11. Celebrity Chat
12. Come Dancing
13. X Factor On Ice
14. Oliver Twist?

Which two programmes could you watch at:

15. 9:30
16. 4:45
17. 2:30
18. 8:20
19. 5:15
20. 6:40
21. 3:30
22. 10:15?

C

What is the total length of the following types of programmes?

1. Local News
2. Quiz Shows
3. Comedy Shows
4. Sport
5. National News
6. Dramas

Which programme would you be watching if you switched channels at the end of:

7. Football
8. Law and Order
9. Merlin
10. Coast
11. Celebrity Chat
12. Oliver Twist

TARGET   To calculate the time taken up by events.

A lesson starts at 1:42.
It finishes at 2:25.
How long does it last?

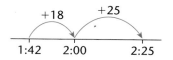

$$18 + 25 = 43$$

Answer *The lesson lasts 43 minutes.*

A

1. Holly gets on a bus at 8:15. She gets off at 8:40. How long is she on the bus?

2. A teacher begins reading a story to her class at 2:25. She finishes at 3:00. How long does it take her to read the story?

3. Playtime begins at 10:30. It ends at 10:50. How long does it last?

4. Terry begins mowing the lawn at 5:05. He finishes at 6:00. How long did it take him?

5. Zoe gets on the London Eye at 12:15. She gets off at 12:45. How long does it take to go round?

6. The cartoons begin at 3:35. They finish at 4:00. How long does the programme last?

B

1. Derek boards the ferry at 2:56. He gets off on the other side of the river at 3:10. How long does the crossing take?

2. Sheri sets off from home at 7:40. She arrives at work at 8:20. How long does her journey take?

3. Colin puts chips in the oven at 5:52. He takes them out at 6:15. How long have they taken to cook?

4. A CD starts to play at 4:35. It finishes at 5:25. How long does the CD last?

5. A coach is due to collect the class at 11:45. It arrives at 12:03. How many minutes late is the coach?

6. Ali gets on a train at 9:25. He gets off at 10:10. How long is he on the train?

7. Beryl goes into the Library at 1:15. She leaves at 2:11. How long has she been in the Library?

C

1. Anna's watch is ten minutes slow. Her watch shows the time as 1:55. What is the actual time?

2. A film lasts 100 minutes. It ends at 8:00. When did it start?

3. It begins to snow at 8:05. The snowfall lasts 85 minutes. When does it stop?

4. Recorder Club begins at 3:23. It finishes at 4:10. How long does it last?

5. A meal takes 50 minutes to cook. It needs to be cooked by 1:15. When should it be put into the oven?

6. The class enter the castle at 10:09. Their visit lasts 1 hour and 45 minutes. When do they leave?

TARGET To solve time problems by calculating lengths of time or by finding start or end times.

A TV programme lasts 43 minutes.
It finishes at 5:15.
When did it start?

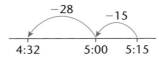

−28   −15

4:32   5:00   5:15

43 − 15 = 28

Answer *The programme started at 4:32.*

A

1. Jon leaves home at 8:25. He arrives at school at 8:50. How long has his journey taken?

2. The Music Lesson begins at 1:45. It finishes at 2:25. How long does it last?

3. Sandy picks up her phone at 9:50. She finishes her call at 10:05. How long does her call take?

4. A television programme starts at 6:55. It finishes at 7:25. How long does it last?

5. Ossie begins making his sandcastle at 11:30. He finishes it at 12:20. How long does it take to make?

6. Cara starts reading her book at 5:35. She finishes it at 6:10. How long has she been reading?

B

1. Harvey leaves the doctor's surgery at 5:18. He has been there for 45 minutes. When did he arrive?

2. Astrid begins writing a letter at 2:45. It takes her 37 minutes to write. When does she finish writing?

3. The sun rises at 7:35 at the start of February. By the end of the month it rises 50 minutes earlier. At what time does the sun rise at the end of February?

4. A wedding ceremony begins at 2:26. It ends at 3:15. How long does it last?

5. A train arrives at 11:05. It is 24 minutes late. When was it due to arrive?

6. Lunchtime starts at 12:15. It lasts 55 minutes. When does it finish?

7. The time on a watch is 4:53. The actual time is 5:09. How many minutes slow is the watch?

C

1. The Computer Club starts at 3:27. It finishes at 4:30. How long does it last?

2. A football match lasts 105 minutes. It finishes at 3:15. When did it start?

3. Anya arrives at the fête at 2:50. She is there for 86 minutes. When does she leave?

4. Javed drives away from his home at 8:35. He stops for petrol at 10:10. How long has he been travelling?

5. Lianne begins cutting her hedge at 11:09. It takes her 83 minutes. When does she finish?

6. Vicki arrives at the airport at 1:25. There is 135 minutes before her plane takes off. When does her plane take off?

TARGET To calculate amounts of money using both £ and p.

Examples
164p = £1·64
309p = £3·09
82p = £0·82
5p = £0·05

BEACH CAFE PRICES

postcard	25p	ice cream	75p	sandwich	£2·50
pen	15p	tea	80p	sunglasses	£3·75
stamps	40p	cake	£1·20		
lolly	35p	cola	55p		

A

Change to pence.

1 £1·60   3 £1·45

2 £2·25   4 £3·90

Change to pounds and pence.

5 230p   7 370p

6 115p   8 255p

Use the above price list. Work out the cost of:

9 2 stamps

10 3 postcards

11 2 lollies

12 3 pens

13 tea, pen

14 ice cream, postcard

15 cola, lolly

16 postcard, pen, stamp

How many of these items could you buy for £1?

17 stamps

18 postcards

19 lollies

20 pens

B

Change to pence.

1 £2.63   3 £5.41

2 £0·97   4 £3.08

Change to pounds and pence.

5 476p   7 4p

6 1000p   8 629p

Use the above price list. Work out the cost of:

9 2 ice creams

10 2 sandwiches

11 sunglasses, lolly

12 tea, cake

13 At the Beach Cafe three teas cost the same as two coffees. What is the cost of one coffee?

14 What different amounts can you make choosing any 3 of these coins?

(10p) (10p) (2p) (50p) (50p)

(10p) (2p) (2p) (50p)

C

Find the cost of these items and the change from £10·00.

1 5 stamps, 5 postcards

2 sunglasses, 2 colas

3 2 teas, 2 cakes

4 sandwich, lolly, pen

5 You buy sunglasses, an ice cream and a pair of flip flops. You pay £10 and receive £3·85 change. How much does the pair of flip flops cost?

6 You buy three colas, a tea and a beach ball. It costs £5·40 altogether. What does the beach ball cost?

7 Find all the different amounts you can make choosing any 3 of these coins.

(£2) (£2) (20p) (20p)
(£1) (£1) (5p) (5p)

TARGET   To add and subtract amounts of money to give change.

SCHOOL FÊTE PRICES

programmes	19p	tea	65p
lucky dip	75p	orange juice	24p
face painting	£2·49	cakes	38p
books	40p	toffee apple	50p
raffle tickets	30p	burgers	£1·25

A

What needs to be added to make 100?

1 50

5 90

2 65

6 45

3 80

7 20

4 15

8 75

Look at the school fête prices above. What would be the change if you buy:

9 3 books for £2

10 tea for £1

11 burger for £2

12 face painting for £3

13 orange for 50p?

14 How many cakes could you buy for £1? How much change would you receive?

15 I have £1. I buy a toffee apple and one other item. I have 31p left. What is the other item?

B

What needs to be added to each number to make 100?

1 63

5 86

2 17

6 54

3 91

7 79

4 38

8 22

Work out the cost of these items and the change from £5.

9 4 programmes

10 burger, 2 teas

11 lucky dip, cake

12 face painting, 2 books

13 Monty buys a burger and one other item for £2. He receives 51p change. What is the other item?

14 Hazel buys ten raffle tickets and one other item for £5. She receives £1·35 change. What is the other item?

15 How many books could you buy for £5? How much change would you receive?

C

What needs to be added to each number to make 1000?

1 480

5 320

2 710

6 560

3 140

7 930

4 670

8 290

Work out the cost of each list and the change from £10.

9 4 burgers
4 raffle tickets
4 oranges

10 programme, tea
face painting, cake

11 Arjun buys 6 books, 3 raffle tickets and one other item for £10. He receives £5·95 change. What is the other item?

12 How many lucky dips can I buy for £10? How much change will I receive?

TARGET To add and subtract amounts of money using written methods.

Examples

```
  £  p
  4 58
+ 2 95
------
  7 53
  1  1
```

```
    7  13 1
    £  p
    6  ⁄4 5
  - 3  7 9
  --------
    2  6 6
```

A
Copy and complete.

1
```
    p
   41
 + 37
```
7
```
    p
   67
 - 35
```

2
```
    p
   28
 + 25
```
8
```
    p
   49
 - 23
```

3
```
    p
   56
 + 44
```
9
```
    p
   94
 - 40
```

4
```
    £
   39
 + 15
```
10
```
    £
   80
 - 56
```

5
```
    £
   47
 + 42
```
11
```
    £
   73
 - 28
```

6
```
    £
   64
 + 27
```
12
```
    £
   52
 - 39
```

13 Pencils cost 29p each. Pens costs 46p more than pencils. How much do pens cost each?

14 Melanie buys two apples and a banana for 77p. The two apples cost 58p altogether. What does the banana cost?

B
Copy and complete.

1
```
   £ p
   2 37
 + 1 56
```
7
```
   £ p
   3 51
 - 2 36
```

2
```
   £ p
   4 82
 +   67
```
8
```
   £ p
   9 37
 - 1 41
```

3
```
   £ p
   3 45
 + 1 89
```
9
```
   £ p
   6 28
 - 2 54
```

4
```
   £ p
   5 61
 + 2 95
```
10
```
   £ p
   7 60
 - 5 29
```

5
```
   £ p
   2 79
 + 2 34
```
11
```
   £ p
   8 42
 - 2 83
```

6
```
   £ p
   4 50
 + 3 68
```
12
```
   £ p
   4 95
 - 1 47
```

13 Cathy buys a burger for £2·35 and a drink for £1·29. How much does she spend altogether?

14 Erik has £7·16. He spends £2·79. How much does he have left?

C
Copy and complete.

1
```
     £
   34·75
 +  6·84
```
7
```
     £
   23·85
 -  7·18
```

2
```
     £
   25·28
 + 17·54
```
8
```
     £
   30·26
 - 14·86
```

3
```
     £
   47·63
 + 22·79
```
9
```
     £
   65·40
 - 45·62
```

4
```
     £
   34·19
 + 19·35
```
10
```
     £
   53·57
 - 23·94
```

5
```
     £
   52·84
 + 43·77
```
11
```
     £
   79·13
 -  7·16
```

6
```
     £
   76·96
 + 18·32
```
12
```
     £
   82·74
 - 36·85
```

13 A pair of headphones costs £42·50. In a sale Steph buys them for £29·79. How much has she saved?

TARGET To solve word problems involving measures.

Example

A hiker walks 15 km every day for 8 days. How far does he walk altogether?

$$
\begin{array}{r}
15 \\
\times \quad 8 \\
\hline
120 \\
\end{array}
$$
₄

Answer
He walks 120 km altogether.

A

1. A van is driven 57 km in the morning and 38 km in the afternoon. How far has it travelled altogether?

2. A full hot water tank holds 100 litres. 46 litres is used. How much hot water is left?

3. What is the total weight of two 25 kg bags of sand?

4. A piece of string is 80 cm long. It is cut into four equal lengths. How long is each length?

5. At high tide a beach is 25 m wide. At low tide it is 37 m wider. How wide is the beach at low tide?

6. A mug holds 200 ml. A paper cup holds 120 ml. How much more does the mug hold than the paper cup?

B

1. A bowl holds 8 litres. It is filled with water 19 times. How much water has been used?

2. Ten identical bags of nuts weigh 650 g altogether. What does one bag weigh?

3. A drink is made using 675 ml of water and 135 ml of squash. How much drink has been made?

4. A large screen TV costs £875. A set with a smaller screen costs £549. How much more does the larger set cost than the smaller set?

5. A field is four times longer than it is wide. It is 73 m wide. How long is the field?

6. There is 84 kg of coal in a bunker. One third is used. How much coal is left?

7. A bottle holds 750 ml of drink. 275 ml is used. How much is left?

C

1. Each bar of chocolate weighs 175 g. What is the total weight of five bars?

2. A the beginning of May a car has a mileage of 7364 miles. At the end of the month it is 8195 miles. How many miles has it been driven during the month?

3. Magnus runs round the playground six times. Altogether he has run 900 m. How far is it once round the playground?

4. There are two paddling pools in the park. The larger one holds 2718 litres. The smaller pool holds 1365 litres. What is the total capacity of the two pools?

5. Each ice cube uses 8 ml of water. How much water is used making 128 cubes?

TARGET   To solve word problems involving measures using mixed units.

Example

A plank is 4 m long
50 cm is cut off.
How long is the plank
which is left?

4 m = 400 cm
400 cm − 50 cm = 350 cm
350 cm = 3 m 50 cm
Answer *3 m 50 cm is left.*

A

1. A bath holds 63 litres of water. 27 litres is cold water. How much hot water went into the bath?

2. It is 70 metres from the classroom to the Hall. Cassie walks there and back. How far has she walked?

3. A small sack of potatoes holds 35 kg. A large sack holds 20 kg more. What is the weight of the potatoes in the large sack?

4. A jug holds 800 ml of milk. It is poured equally into four glasses. How much milk is in each glass?

5. Freda Frog jumps 84 cm. Freddie jumps 67 cm. How much further does Freda jump?

6. One bar of soap weighs 60 g. What is the total weight of three bars?

B

1. Each packet of jelly weighs 200 g. What do ten packets weigh in kilograms?

2. It is 2 km from Rahul's home to school. Trevor lives 700 m closer. How far is it from Trevor's home to school?

3. There is 300 ml of water in a saucepan. Half a litre is added. How much water is in the saucepan?

4. A row of five tiles is one metre long. What is the length of each tile?

5. A packet of sugar weighs one kilogram. 400 g is used. How much is left?

6. Bottles of washing up liquid hold 400 ml. How much liquid is in six bottles altogether? Give your answer in litres and millilitres.

C

1. Tina is one and a quarter metres tall. Her mother is 48 cm taller. How tall is Tina's mother?

2. One quarter of a litre bottle of milk is used. How much is left?

3. In five minutes Gloria can run 850 m. In the same time she can cycle twice as far. How far can she cycle in five minutes? Give your answer in kilometres and metres.

4. To feed the birds in his garden, Andy buys three quarters of a kilogram of seed and 500 g of peanuts. What is the total weight of the bird food?

5. A kettle holds one and a half litres of water. 900 ml is used. How much water is left?

6. Five identical bricks weigh 8 kg. What does one brick weigh?

TARGET To solve word problems involving measures mentally.

Example

A stack of four building blocks is 32 cm tall. How thick is each block?

$32 \div 4 = 8$

Answer
Each block is 8 cm thick.

A

1. Tim has 50p. He spends 20p. How much does he have left?

2. Rosa puts four 10 g weights on a balance. How much weight is on the balance?

3. A shower uses 20 litres of water. A bath uses 40 litres more. How much water is used in a bath?

4. A sack of potatoes weighs 25 kg. 7 kg is eaten. How much is left?

5. A garden is 40 m long. A lawn stretches half the length of the garden. How long is the lawn?

6. Jeff has £8. Asif has £5 more than Jeff. How much do they have altogether?

B

1. Tickets for a coach trip cost £6 each. How much will four tickets cost?

2. A small can of oil holds 90 ml. A large can holds 70 ml more. How much oil is in the large can?

3. A large packet of cornflakes holds 800 g. A small packet holds 500 g. How much more is in the large packet?

4. How many 3 cm strips can be cut from 24 cm of tape?

5. Abbie travels 73 km by train and a further 11 km by bus. How far has she travelled altogether?

6. Lance buys a lolly for 70p. He pays £1. How much change is he given?

C

1. Anika has a 1 kg bag of flour. She uses 450 g. How much flour is left?

2. Emily has seven 50p coins. How much money does she have altogether?

3. Joel drove a car 238 m. Kevin drove the car 7 m further. How long was Kevin's drive?

4. A ribbon is 75 cm long. Nicole cuts off 19 cm. How much ribbon is left?

5. One litre of lemonade is poured into four equal glasses. How much lemonade is in each glass?

6. One can of cola holds 350 ml. How much cola is there in two cans?

TARGET To solve word problems involving the multiplication or division of measures mentally.

Examples

A bottle holds 800 ml of juice.
One half is used. How much juice is left?

800 ml ÷ 2 = 400 ml

Answer *400 ml of juice is left.*

How many seconds are there in 5 minutes?

60 secs. × 5 = 300 secs.

Answer *300 seconds in 5 minutes.*

A

1. The halfway point of a cycle race is 40 km. How long is the race?

2. How many hours are there in a quarter of a day?

3. Russ sprinkles five litres of water on his plants every day. How much water does he use in a week?

4. A pipe is 90 cm long. One third is cut off. How long are the two pieces?

5. One biscuit weighs 10 g. What do ten biscuits weigh?

6. Carol's pen weighs 18 g. Her pencil weighs half as much. What is the weight of Carol's pencil?

B

1. One side of a square tile is 25 cm long. What is the length of a row of four tiles?

2. Eight bags of crisps weigh 240 g altogether. What does one bag weigh?

3. How many minutes are there in three hours?

4. There is 500 ml of paint in a can. One tenth is used. How much paint has been used?

5. Five lengths of a swimming pool is 150 m. How long is the pool?

6. Eighteen litres of water is lost from a dripping tap every day. How much water is lost in two days?

C

1. Each bar of chocolate weighs 75 g. How much do twenty bars weigh?

2. How many hours are there in five days?

3. Penny runs round the garden seven times. Altogether she runs 560 m. What is the distance round Penny's garden?

4. A greengrocer has 72 kg of potatoes. One quarter of the potatoes is sold. How much is left?

5. A jug holds 1200 ml of orange juice. It is poured equally into six glasses. How much juice is in each glass?

TARGET To solve word problems involving the multiplication or division of measures mentally.

Examples

Four identical rubbers weigh 120 g altogether. What does one rubber weigh?

$$120 g \div 4 = 30 g$$

Answer *One rubber weighs 30 g.*

One train ticket costs £40. What do 5 tickets cost?

$$£40 \times 5 = £200$$

Answer *5 tickets cost £200.*

A

1. There is 25 kg of sand in one bag. How much sand is there in three bags?

2. Bella puts six 20 g weights on a balance. How much weight is on the balance altogether?

3. A bus makes the same journey ten times in a day. It travels 270 km altogether. How long is the journey?

4. Glasgow received 180 cm of rain in one year. Manchester had half as much. How much rain fell in Manchester in that year?

5. A bath is filled using 17 litres of cold water and four times as much hot water. How much hot water is used in the bath?

B

1. A pot of cream holds 300 ml. One half is used. How much cream is left?

2. One coin weighs 15 g. What is the weight of eight coins?

3. Jane buys a painting for £150. She pays with £20 notes. How many will she need?

4. A carton of apple juice holds 400 ml. The juice is poured equally into five glasses. How much juice is in each glass?

5. A fence round the outside of a square field is 240 m long. What is the length of the field?

6. Elvis buys his newspaper for 50p every day for a week. How much has he spent?

7. Monica has a 50 cm length of wood. How many 8 cm lengths can she cut from her wood?

C

1. Each portion of cereal is 30 g. How many portions can be served from a 700 g packet?

2. A running track is 400 m long. Gordon runs round the track four times. How far has he run altogether?

3. Sameera walks 6 km every day. How many days will it take her to walk 100 km?

4. Frank takes 20 ml of medicine every day for two weeks. How much medicine does he take altogether?

5. Each new house will be built in a plot of land 12 m wide. How many houses can be built along one side of a road 80 m long?

6. One flapjack weighs 65 g. What do nine flapjacks weigh?

TARGET   To draw 2-D shapes.

Right angles are marked. Use square paper or a set square to draw right angles accurately.
All lengths are in centimetres.

Examples   3 = 3 cm   4·5 = 4 cm 5 mm   2·7 = 2 cm 7 mm

A

Construct each shape and check that the opposite sides are equal.

1

2

3
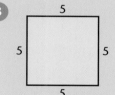

4
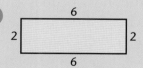

The perimeter of a shape is the distance around its edges.

Example   The perimeter of the above rectangle is:

(6 + 2 + 6 + 2) cm = 16 cm

5   Construct a shape with a perimeter of 28 cm.

6   Construct a rectangle with a perimeter of 18 cm and a longest side of 5 cm.

B

Construct each shape and measure the length of the diagonal to the nearest mm.

1
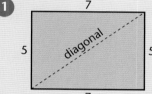

2
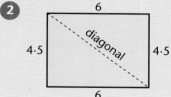

3   A square with a perimeter of 10 cm.

4   A rectangle with a perimeter of 17 cm and a shortest side of 4 cm.

Construct each triangle and measure the length of the longest side to the nearest mm.

5

6
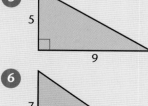

C

Construct each shape and measure the length of the diagonal.

1
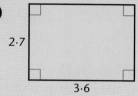

2   A rectangle with a perimeter of 14·8 cm and a shortest side of 2·6 cm.

3   Construct each triangle and measure all unmarked sides.

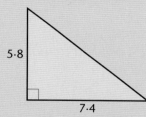

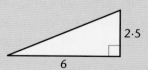

4   Construct the quadrilateral. Find the length of side *x*.

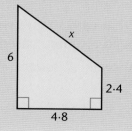

TARGET   To make 3-D shapes.

USING CUBES

Example
How many cubes
are needed to build
this cuboid?

2 layers of cubes
6 cubes in each layer
Answer   *12 cubes are needed.*

DRAWING NETS
3-D shapes with straight edges can be made
by drawing 2-D nets.

Example
Which of these nets will fold to make an
open cube?

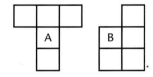

Answer
*Net A will fold to make an open cube, but Net
B will not.*

USING STRAWS OR CARD
3-D shapes can be made by joining straws
for edges or flat pieces of card for faces.

Example
1 How many lengths of straw are needed
   to build a cuboid?
   Answer   *12*

2 What card shapes would you need to
   build a square based pyramid?
   Answer   *1 square, 4 triangles*

A

1 How many cubes are needed to
   build this cuboid?

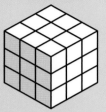

2 Use cubes to build the cuboid.
   Were you right?

3 **a)** How many cubes are needed to
        build this cuboid?

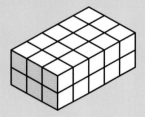

   b) Build the cuboid.
        Were you right?

4 Use the same number of cubes as
   you needed to build the second
   cuboid. Build a different cuboid
   which also has a height of 2 cubes.
   Write down the length and width of
   the cuboid.

5 Use 32 cubes.
   Find three different cuboids with a
   height of 2 cubes. Write down the
   length and width of each cuboid.

6 Use 8 cubes.
   Build a cube. Write down the length,
   width and height of your cube.

B

1 How many cubes would be needed to build this cuboid? (Lengths in cubes.)

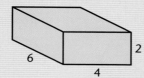

2 Find other cuboids you could build using this number of cubes. Write down the length, width and height of each cuboid.

3 Copy these nets onto squared paper. Cut them out and fold them to make open cubes.

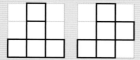

4 Find different nets that make open cubes.

5 How many lengths of straw would you need to build:
a) a cube
b) a triangular prism
c) a square based pyramid
d) a triangular based pyramid?

6 How many flat pieces of card would you need to build:
a) a cuboid
b) a triangular prism
c) a triangular based pyramid
d) a pentagonal prism?

7 How many 1 cm cubes would you need to build a cube with edges 4 cm long?

C

1 How many cubes would be needed to build each cuboid? (Lengths in cubes.)

a)

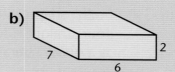

b)

2 Copy this net onto squared paper. Cut it out and fold it to make a closed cube.

3 Find different nets that make closed cubes.

4 Copy this net onto one centimetre squared paper. Cut it out to make a square based pyramid with a height of 5 cm.

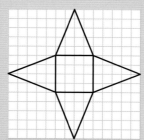

5 Draw a net for each of the cuboids in question **1**.

6 How many 1 cm cubes would you need to build a cube with edges:
a) 5 cm long   **b)** 10 cm long?

TARGET To recognise and describe 2-D shapes.

A 2-D shape with straight edges is a polygon. Shapes with curved edges are non-polygons.

POLYGONS   NON-POLYGONS

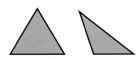

A 2-D shape with three straight sides is a triangle.

A 2-D shape with four straight sides is a quadrilateral. Squares are quadrilaterals.

Other polygons include:
5 sides – pentagon
6 sides – hexagon
8 sides – octagon

A circle, a semi-circle and a sector of a circle are non-polygons.

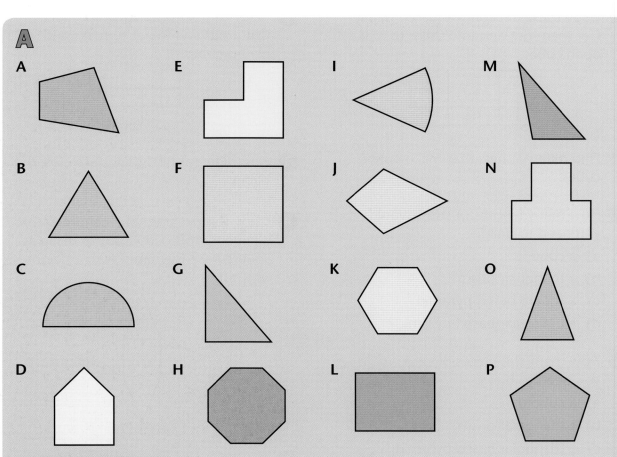

Look at the above shapes.

1 Write the letter and name of the two shapes with curved edges.

2 For each of the shapes with straight edges write:
   a) the letter
   b) the number of sides
   c) the name of the shape.

B

Look at the shapes in Section A.
Give the letter of the following shapes:

1 a quadrilateral with four right angles and two pairs of equal sides

2 a triangle which is symmetrical but does not have all sides equal

3 a hexagon which is symmetrical

4 a pentagon with all sides equal

5 a non-polygon with one straight side

6 a shape with four pairs of equal sides

7 a quadrilateral with no right angle and two pairs of equal sides

8 a triangle with all its sides equal

9 a pentagon with three right angles

10 a triangle with an obtuse angle

11 a hexagon with all sides equal

12 a right-angled triangle

13 a quadrilateral with three obtuse angles and no equal sides

14 a non-polygon with two straight sides

15 a quadrilateral with four equal sides

16 an octagon with not all sides equal

17

Which shape is the odd one out?
Give a reason for your answer.

C

Look at the shapes in Section A.
Give the letter of all the shapes which:

1 have 6 or more sides

2 have 2 or more right angles

3 have no line of symmetry

4 have 2 or more pairs of parallel sides

5 are quadrilaterals with no right angle

6 are non-polygons

7 have more than one line of symmetry

8 have 2 or more acute angles.

9 Copy the Carroll diagram.
Sort the shapes in Section A by writing the letters in the right places.

	more than 4 sides	not more than 4 sides
symmetrical		
not symmetrical		

10

A   B   C   D

Class 3 were asked to choose the odd one out from these four shapes. Chris chose B. Molly chose D. They were both able to give a good reason for their choice.
What were the two reasons given?

TARGET   To recognise and describe 3-D shapes.

CURVED EDGES
These 3-D shapes
have curved edges.

sphere	cone
hemisphere	cylinder

STRAIGHT EDGES
A 3-D shape with straight edges is a polyhedron.
These shapes are polyhedra (plural of polyhedron).

cube	triangular based pyramid
cuboid	triangular prism
square based pyramid	

Examples

cylinder

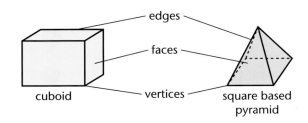
cuboid   square based pyramid

A

Here are some shapes.

A 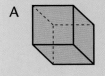   B   C   D 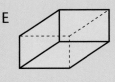   E

F   G   H    I

Write down the letter of:

1. 3 shapes with a circular face

2. 2 shapes with a square face

3. 1 shape with 4 vertices

4. 1 shape with no flat faces

5. 3 shapes with a triangular face

6. 3 shapes with curved edges

7. 2 shapes with 12 edges

8. 2 shapes with five faces

9. 2 shapes with one circular face

10. 2 shapes with rectangular faces

11. 1 shape with six edges

12. 1 shape with six vertices.

B

1 Look at the shapes in Section A.
Write the letter and name of each shape in order from A to I.

2 Copy and complete this table showing the number of faces, edges and vertices for each of the polyhedra shown in Section A.

Name of shape	Number of faces	Number of edges	Number of vertices
cube			
square based pyramid			
triangular prism			
triangular based pyramid			
cuboid			

C

A prism is a polyhedron with two identical end faces and the same cross-section throughout its length.

Examples

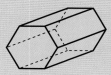

pentagonal (5 sided) based prism

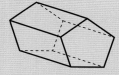

hexagonal (6-sided) based prism

1 For each of the above prisms list the number of:

   a) faces   **b)** edges   **c)** vertices

2 Which three shapes in Section A are prisms?

Name the odd one out in each group. Give a reason for your choice.

3   **4**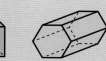

5   **6**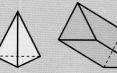

7 Explain why each shape in this group could be the odd one out.

TARGET To recognise half turns, three quarter turns and whole turns as numbers of right angles.

$\frac{1}{4}$ turn right angle	half turn 2 right angles	three quarters turn 3 right angles	whole turn 4 right angles
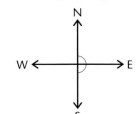			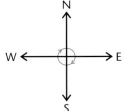

A

Find the new time if the hour hand:

makes a $\frac{1}{2}$ turn

1. from 12:00
2. from 3:00
3. from 9:00
4. from 6:00

turns a right angle

5. from 3:00
6. from 9:00
7. from 6:00
8. from 12:00

Are these compass movements half turns or right angles?

9. W to N
10. N to S
11. S to W
12. E to W

13. N to E
14. W to E
15. E to S
16. S to N

B

In which direction would you be facing?

Make a $\frac{1}{4}$ turn:

1. right from E
2. left from N
3. right from S
4. left from W
5. right from N
6. left from S

Make a $\frac{3}{4}$ turn:

7. left from N
8. right from E
9. left from S
10. right from N
11. left from W
12. right from W

Find the new time. The hour hand turns:

13. a half turn from 10 o'clock
14. a whole turn from 2 o'clock
15. a 3 quarters turn from 8 o'clock
16. a quarter turn from 11 o'clock
17. a half turn from 1 o'clock
18. a 3 quarters turn from 4 o'clock.

C

Angles are measured in degrees (°).
A whole turn is 360°.
A right angle is 90°.

Find the new time. The hour hand turns:

1. 180° from 5
2. 270° from 11
3. 360° from 7
4. 180° from 8

5. 90° from 2
6. 30° from 2
7. 90° from 7
8. 60° from 7

How many degrees is the clockwise turn from:

9. W to N
10. E to W
11. S to E
12. N to E

13. SW to NE
14. SE to S
15. W to NW
16. NE to NW

TARGET To identify right angles and whether angles are greater or less than right angles.

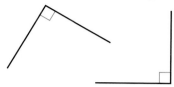

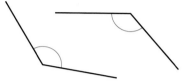

right angle | less than a right angle (an acute angle) | greater than a right angle (an obtuse angle)

A

Use a set square.
Decide if each angle is:

a) a right angle
b) less than a right angle
c) greater than a right angle.

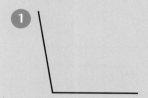
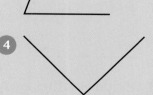

B

Use a set square.
Decide if each angle is:

a) a right angle
b) less than a right angle
c) greater than a right angle.

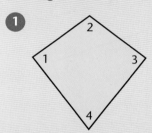
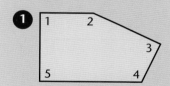

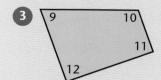
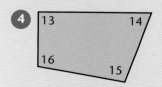

5 Draw a triangle with one angle greater than a right angle.

C

Do not use a set square.
Decide if each angle is:

a) an acute angle
b) a right angle
c) an obtuse angle
d) greater than a half turn.

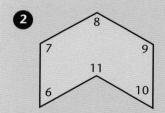
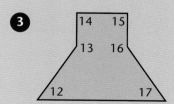

4 Draw a quadrilateral with two angles greater than a right angle.

TARGET To identify right angles, acute angles and obtuse angles in shapes.

RIGHT ANGLES
right angles are
a quarter turn

ACUTE ANGLES
less than a
quarter turn

OBTUSE ANGLES
greater than a
quarter turn

A

Decide if each angle is:
a) a right angle
b) an acute angle
c) an obtuse angle.

1

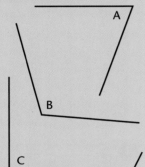

2 Use a set square to check.

B

Decide whether each of the angles of these shapes is:
a) a right angle
b) an acute angle
c) an obtuse angle.

1
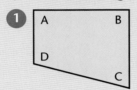

2
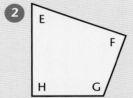

3
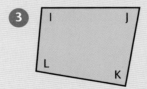

4
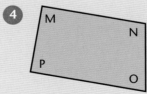

5
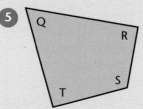

6 Use a set square to check.

C

Write the angles of each shape in order of size, smallest first.

1
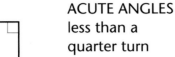

2
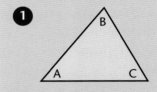

3
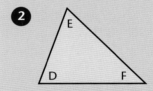

4
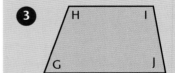

5
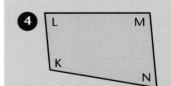

6 Decide whether each of the above angles A to R is acute, obtuse or a right angle.

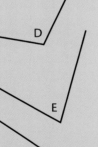
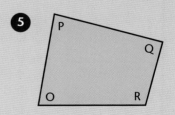

TARGET To identify horizontal and vertical lines.

Example

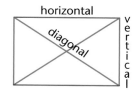

horizontal
diagonal
vertical

In the diagram:
horizontal lines are red
vertical lines are blue
diagonal lines are green.

A

Copy the shapes.
Use one colour for all the horizontal lines.
Use a second colour for all the vertical lines.
Use a pencil for all other lines.

1 2 3 4 5 6 7 8 9 10 11 12

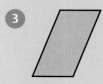
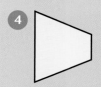
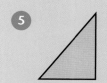
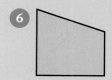

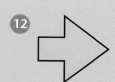

B

Use squared paper.
Copy each flag in a 6 × 4 grid. Use one colour pen to show all the horizontal lines.
Use a different colour pen for all the vertical lines.

1 2 3 4 5

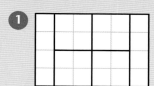
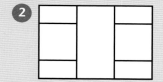
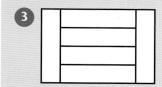
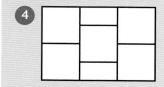
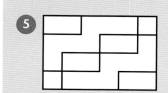

C

Use squared paper.
Copy each flag in a 6 × 4 grid.
Use different colours to show:
a) all the horizontal lines
b) all the vertical lines
c) all the diagonal lines.

1 2 3 4 5

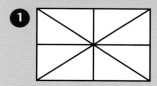
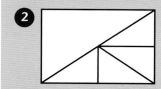
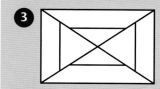

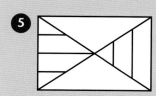

TARGET   To identify parallel and perpendicular lines.

Lines are parallel if they would never meet even if continued forever. They are shown with arrows.

Lines are perpendicular if they cross at right angles.

Example

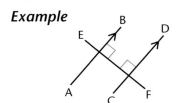

AB and CD are parallel.

EF is perpendicular to both AB and CD.

A

Example

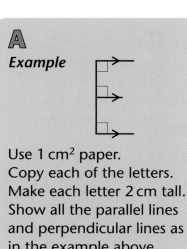

Use 1 cm² paper.
Copy each of the letters.
Make each letter 2 cm tall.
Show all the parallel lines and perpendicular lines as in the example above.

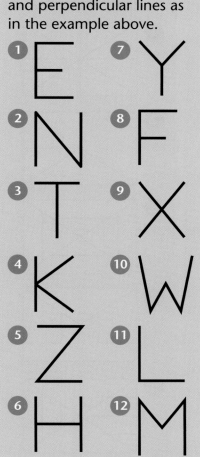

1 E   **7** Y

2 N   **8** F

3 T   **9** X

4 K   **10** W

5 Z   **11** L

6 H   **12** M

B

Copy the following shapes. Show pairs of parallel and perpendicular sides as in the example above.

1

2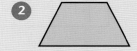

3

4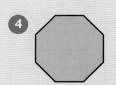

5

6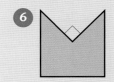

C

Copy and complete each sentence by writing *parallel* or *perpendicular* in the space.

1 AB is .... to BC.

2 AD is .... to BC.

3 AC is .... to BD.

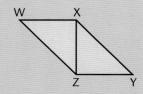

Copy and complete by writing the missing line.

4 WX is parallel to ....

5 YZ is perpendicular to ....

6 XY is parallel to ....

7 Use squared paper.
Using the intersections of grids of 4 squares make different polygons with more than 3 sides.
Show pairs of parallel and perpendicular sides.

Example
Pentagon

TARGET   To solve problems involving mental addition and subtraction.

In a magic square the sum of each row, column and diagonal is the same.

15	8	7
2	10	18
13	12	5

Examples

Row $15 + 8 + 7 = 30$
Column $7 + 18 + 5 = 30$
Diagonal $13 + 10 + 7 = 30$

Copy and complete the following magic squares.

A

1

3		
7	6	
8		

2

		8
	5	
2	7	

3

	7	
10	9	5

4

11		
	10	
17		9

5

		10
		5
4		6

B

1

8		12
		5
		10

2

6	11	16
15		

3

5		
	12	3
		19

4

	9	22
	14	
6		

5

25		
	50	
40		75

C

1

13	22	10
	15	

2

14		16
	20	
		26

3

8	33	
	17	
	1	

4

		11
18	22	
33		

5

		22
16	17	24

TARGET To present data in pictograms.

A pictogram shows data (information) in symbols.
A key explains what the symbol means.

Example

This table shows the number of portions of each of the different fish sold in a fish and chip shop.

The data in the table is presented below in a pictogram.

Fish	Numbers of portions
cod	14
haddock	12
mackerel	16
plaice	8
salmon	10

cod

haddock

mackerel

plaice

salmon

represents 2 fish

A

1 This table shows the colours of cars in a school car park.

Colours	Number of cars
black	5
blue	1
grey	7
red	2
silver	4
white	6

Draw a vertical pictogram to show the results.

2 The children in Class 3 chose their favourite ice cream flavours.

Flavour	Votes
chocolate	6
coffee	3
mint	8
strawberry	4
toffee	2
vanilla	5

Draw a horizontal pictogram to show the results.

B

1 This table shows the number of pairs of shoes owned by six adults.

Name	Pairs of shoes
Adele	6
Bill	12
Candy	14
Dennis	4
Eve	10
Floyd	8

Draw a vertical pictogram to show the results. Let each picture represent 2 pairs of shoes.

2 This table shows the numbers of the different types of trees found in a wood.

Trees	Numbers in wood
Ash	20
Beech	80
Elm	30
Horsechestnut	50
Oak	60
Yew	40

Draw a horizontal pictogram to show the results. Use a scale of one picture to represent 10 trees.

C

1 The number of sunny days in each of the first six months of the year.

Month	Days
January	8
February	6
March	12
April	14
May	18
June	20

Draw a horizontal pictogram to show the data. Use a scale of one symbol to represent 4 days. Use half a symbol to represent 2 days.

2 The number of fish caught on a boat in one week at sea.

Days	Fish
Sunday	350
Monday	125
Tuesday	275
Wednesday	400
Thursday	175
Friday	200
Saturday	325

Draw a vertical pictogram to show the results, using a scale of one symbol to represent 50 fish.

TARGET To use information presented in pictograms.

Example

This pictogram shows the number of arrows striking the different colours of an archery target during a competition.

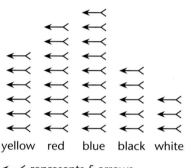

yellow   red   blue   black   white

⟵< represents 5 arrows

Look at the pictogram.

1. How many actual arrows are shown by one arrow symbol?
5 actual arrows

2. How many arrows struck the yellow ring? *30*

3. Which colour was struck least often?
white

4. Which ring was struck 40 times?
red

5. How many more times was the blue ring struck than the black? *20*

A

This pictogram shows the number of days it rained in each month.

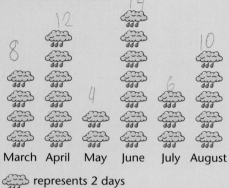

March   April   May   June   July   August

☁ represents 2 days

1. Which month had the most days of rain?

2. Which month had the least number of rainy days?

3. How many days did it rain in:
   a) March   **b)** August?

4. Which month had 12 days during which it rained?

5. How many more days did it rain in June than in July?

6. How many more days did it rain in April than in May?

7. How many days did it rain altogether in the three summer months of June, July and August?

8. How many days did it rain in the three spring months of March, April and May altogether?

9. How many more days did it rain in the summer than in the spring?

B

Six children took part in a general knowledge quiz. There were 50 questions altogether. This pictogram shows how many each child answered correctly.

Ahmed	✓ ✓ ✓ ✓ ✓ ✓
Tania	✓ ✓ ✓
Kate	✓ ✓ ✓ ✓ ✓
Shane	✓ ✓ ✓ ✓ ✓ ✓ ✓
Dan	✓ ✓ ✓ ✓
Julie	✓ ✓ ✓ ✓ ✓ ✓ ✓ ✓

✓ represents 5 correct answers

1. Who got the most questions right?

2. Who answered the least number of questions correctly?

3. How many questions were answered correctly by:
   a) Shane   b) Dan?

4. Who got:
   a) 30 questions right
   b) 45 questions right?

5. How many more did Ahmed answer correctly than Tania?

6. How many less questions did Dan get right than Julie?

7. How many questions were answered wrongly by:
   a) Ahmed   b) Tania?

C

This pictogram shows the number of tents at a campsite each day in one week in August.

Sunday	△ △ △ △ △ ⟋
Monday	△ △ △
Tuesday	△ ⟋
Wednesday	△ △
Thursday	△ △ △ ⟋
Friday	△ △ △ △ △
Saturday	△ △ △ △ △ △ ⟋

△ represents 10 tents

1. On which day was there:
   a) the largest number of tents
   b) the smallest number of tents?

2. On which day were there:
   a) 15 tents   b) 40 tents?

3. How many tents were there on:
   a) Wednesday   b) Sunday?

4. How many more tents were there on Monday than on Tuesday?

5. How many fewer tents were there on Friday than on Saturday?

6. The campsite fee for a tent pitch is £10 per night. How much was taken in site fees during the week?

TARGET To present data in a bar chart.

Example

This table shows the number of passengers getting on each of the five buses stopping at a bus stop.

Bus	Numbers of passengers
Bus 1	16
Bus 2	8
Bus 3	18
Bus 4	10
Bus 5	14

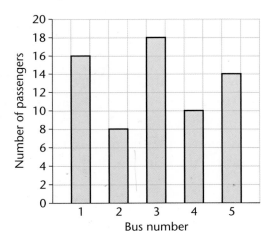

The number of passengers getting on each bus can be presented in a bar chart.

A

1. This table shows the puddings chosen by the children in one class at lunchtime.

Pudding	Children
trifle	4
crumble	8
brownie	5
yogurt	0
ice cream	9
fruit	2

Draw a bar chart to show the data.

2. This table shows the number of hours of sunshine each day during one week in June.

Days	Sunshine hours
Sunday	9
Monday	4
Tuesday	1
Wednesday	7
Thursday	0
Friday	10
Saturday	6

Draw a bar chart to show the information.

B

1 The children in a school were allowed to vote for the colour of the new PE vest. These are the results of the vote.

Vest colour	Votes
blue	40
green	5
pink	50
red	20
white	35
yellow	25
others	10

Draw a bar chart to show the results. Label the bar chart in fives.

2 Six children timed how long it took them to walk to school. These are the results.

Name	Time (minutes)
Dean	18
Karl	12
Kerry	6
Maya	16
Marcus	22
Sharee	10

Draw a bar chart labelled in twos to show the results.

C

1 Sinead wanted to know how long the words were in her reading book. She looked at the first 400 words. These are the results of her investigation.

Number of Letters	Number of Words
1	10
2	65
3	95
4	125
5	35
6	30
7	15
8	10
Over 8	15

Draw a bar chart to show Sinead's results. Label the bar chart in tens.

2 A company manufacturing dog food wanted to know which breed of dog to have on their cans. They asked 1000 people to name their favourite breed. These are the results.

Breed	Votes
Beagle	130
Boxer	80
German Shepherd	170
Golden Retriever	160
Labrador	210
Yorkshire Terrier	140
Others	110

Draw a bar chart labelled in twenties to show the results of the survey.

TARGET   To solve problems using information presented in bar charts.

Example

This bar chart shows the lengths of the stories written by five children.

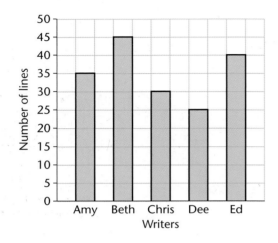

Look at the bar chart.

1. What is the value of one division (square)?   *5 lines*

2. How many lines did Amy write?   *35 lines*

3. Who wrote the least number of lines?   *Dee*

4. Who wrote 40 lines?   *Ed*

5. How many more lines were written by Beth than by Chris?   *15 (45 − 30)*

A

This bar chart shows the ages of children at a birthday party.

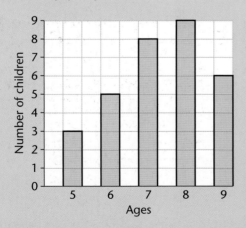

1. How old was the youngest person at the party?

2. How old was the oldest child?

3. How many of the children were 7?

4. What was the most common age?

5. How many more children were 8 than 9?

6. How many fewer children were 5 than 6?

7. How many more children were 7 than 9?

8. How many children were at the party altogether?

9. How many of the children were less than 7 years old?

10. How many children were older than 8?

B

This bar chart shows the audience at the afternoon performance of a film during the Christmas Holiday.

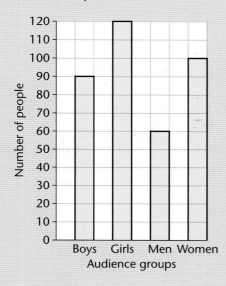

1. How many girls were in the audience?

2. How many men watched the film?

3. How many fewer boys were there than girls?

4. How many more women were there than men?

5. How many children were there altogether?

6. How many adults were in the audience?

7. What was the total size of the audience?

8. How many more members of the audience were female than male?

C

This bar chart shows the number of apples picked at an orchard each day for one week.

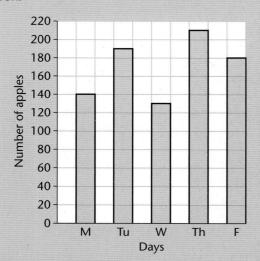

1. On which day were most apples picked?

2. On which day were the least apples picked?

3. On which day were:
   a) 180 apples picked
   b) 130 apples picked?

4. How many apples were picked on:
   a) Monday   b) Thursday?

5. How many more apples were picked on Tuesday than on Monday?

6. How many fewer apples were picked on Wednesday than on Thursday?

7. How many apples were picked in the week altogether?

8. How many fewer apples were picked on the first two days of the week than on the last two days?

TARGET To solve problems using information presented in bar charts.

Example

This bar chart shows the colours of cars sold at a showroom.

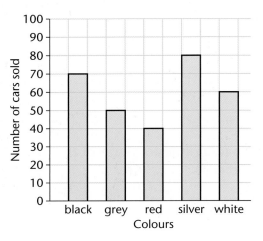

Look at the bar chart.

1. What is the value of one division (square)? *10 cars*

2. How many black cars were sold? *70*

3. Which colour was sold most often? *silver*

4. Cars of which colour were sold 60 times? *white*

5. How many more black cars were sold than grey cars? *20 (70 − 50)*

6. How many fewer red cars than silver cars were sold? *40 (80 − 40)*

A

Three children wanted to find out how many paper clips their magnets would pick up. They tested five different magnets which they labelled A–E. They presented their results in a bar chart.

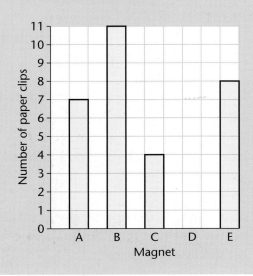

1. Which magnet picked up the most paper clips?

2. Which magnet did not pick up any clips?

3. Which magnet picked up 8 clips?

4. How many clips were picked up by Magnet C?

5. How many fewer clips were picked up by:

   a) Magnet A than Magnet B

   b) Magnet D than Magnet E?

6. How many more clips were picked up by:

   a) Magnet B than Magnet E

   b) Magnet A than Magnet C?

B

The school weather station measures the rainfall all year. The total rainfall for each season in one full year is shown in the bar chart.

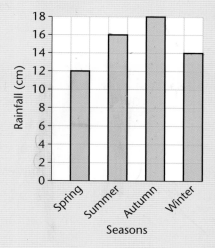

1. Which season had the most rain?

2. Which season had the least rain?

3. How much rain fell in the winter?

4. Which season had 16 cm of rain?

5. How much less rain fell in the winter than the summer?

6. How much more rain fell in the autumn than the spring?

7. How much rain fell in the year altogether?

8. How much less rain fell in the 6 months of spring and summer than in the next 6 months?

C

The children in Class 3 investigated how far away from the school they lived. This horizontal bar chart shows the results for the children on Blue Table.

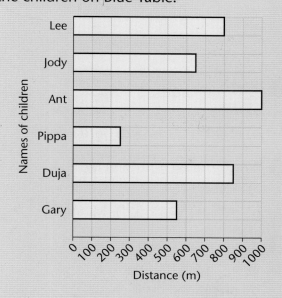

1.

2.

3.

4.

P. 127 C

high adventure

5. How much further from the school is Lee than Jody?

6. How much nearer to the school is Gary than Duja?

7. Ant walks to school but goes back to Gary's house. How far has he walked altogether?

8. How far do each of the children walk going to and from school each day in kilometres?

TARGET To solve problems using information presented in tables.

This table shows the lunch choices of 12 children on a school trip.
Each child chose one of the 3 available choices for each item.

NAME	COACH SEAT	SANDWICH	DRINK	CAKE	FRUIT
Erin	1	peanut butter	mango	muffin	grapes
William	2	turkey	orange	brownie	banana
Ameera	3	cheese	orange	brownie	grapes
Lance	4	turkey	mango	muffin	banana
Minnie	5	peanut butter	mango	fairy cake	grapes
Camille	6	peanut butter	apple	brownie	apple
Jordan	7	cheese	mango	muffin	apple
Alfie	8	turkey	mango	brownie	grapes
Lynda	9	peanut butter	orange	brownie	banana
Ryan	10	turkey	orange	fairy cake	banana
Tyrone	11	peanut butter	orange	muffin	grapes
Courtney	12	cheese	mango	brownie	apple

A

Look at the table.

1 Who was sitting at seat number:
   a) 3
   b) 11
   c) 6
   d) 4?

2 What was the seat number of:
   a) Lynda
   b) William
   c) Alfie
   d) Courtney?

3 What sandwich was chosen by:
   a) Erin
   b) Jordan
   c) Ryan
   d) Minnie?

4 Which drink was chosen by:
   a) Lance
   b) Camille
   c) Lynda
   d) Erin?

5 Which cake was chosen by:
   a) Alfie
   b) Ryan
   c) Ameera
   d) Jordan?

6 Which fruit was chosen by:
   a) Tyrone
   b) William
   c) Courtney
   d) Minnie?

7 How many children chose:
   a) a cheese sandwich
   b) an orange drink
   c) grapes
   d) a muffin?

8 Which two children chose a fairy cake?

B

Look at the table on page 128.

1 What was the most popular choice of:

  a) cake   **b)** fruit?

2 What was the least popular choice of:

  a) drink   **b)** sandwich?

3 How many more children chose:

  a) grapes than an apple

  b) a mango drink than an orange drink

  c) a muffin than a fairy cake

  d) a peanut butter sandwich than a turkey sandwich?

4 How many fewer children chose:

  a) a muffin than a brownie

  b) a turkey sandwich than a peanut butter sandwich

  c) an apple drink than an orange drink

  d) a banana than grapes?

5 Who chose a cheese sandwich and an orange drink?

6 Who chose an orange drink and a muffin?

7 Who chose a muffin and an apple?

8 Who chose the same sandwich and drink as Tyrone?

9 Who chose the same cake and fruit as Ameera?

10 How many children chose a turkey sandwich and a mango drink?

11 How many children chose a fairy cake and an apple?

C

Look at the table on page 128.

1 Who chose a mango drink and a banana?

2 Who chose a turkey sandwich and grapes?

3 Who chose the same sandwich and cake as Erin?

4 Who chose the same drink, cake and fruit as Lynda?

5 Which two people chose both the least popular sandwich and the least popular fruit?

6 What was the most popular combination of sandwich and fruit?

7 How many children chose the same drink and cake as Jordan?

8 Which children chose both the most popular cake and the most popular fruit?

9 Copy and complete the bar chart, dividing each bar to show the number of choices for each item.

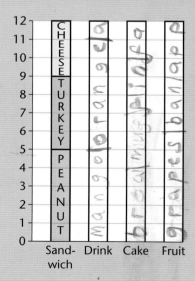

10 What would you have chosen?

Write each of the numbers in figures.

1. six hundred and fifty-one

2. two hundred and ninety

3. three hundred and seven

4. four hundred and eighty-two

Write each of the numbers in words.

5. 385

9. 402

6. 714

10. 839

7. 260

11. 146

8. 597

12. 973

13. Use these digits.

 9 3 6

Make all the possible three-digit numbers. Write each of the three-digit numbers:

a) in figures

b) in words.

Give the value of the underlined digit.

14. 3<u>7</u>9

18. 9<u>8</u>6

15. <u>5</u>31

19. 46<u>5</u>

16. 728<u>8</u>

20. 89<u>2</u>

17. <u>2</u>04

21. 6<u>9</u>3

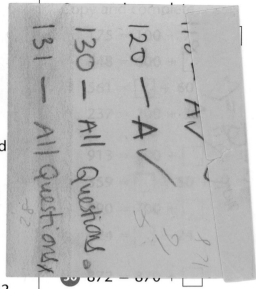

30. 872 = 870 + ☐

31. 205 = ☐ + 5

32. 687 = 680 + ☐

33. 153 = ☐ + 3

Which number is smaller?

34. 225 or 252

35. 943 or 934

36. 584 or 548

37. 169 or 196

Which number is larger?

38. 491 or 419

39. 752 or 725

40. 628 or 682

41. 317 or 371

Write in order, smallest number first.

42. 835   358   853   583

43. 274   427   472   247

44. 210   120   102   201

45. 435   453   345   354

Start at 0.
What number do you reach if you count:

46. six steps of 4

47. seven steps of 5

48. twelve steps of 2

49. ten steps of 10

50. eight steps of 3

51. five steps of 8

52. four steps of 50

53. nine steps of 100?

Copy the sequence.
Write the next four numbers.

54. 94   95   96   97

55. 153   143   133   123

56. 71   171   271   371

57. 706   606   506   406

Work out

58. 547 + 10

59. 295 + 10

60. 906 + 10

61. 438 − 10

62. 671 − 10

63. 804 − 10

64. 123 + 100

65. 362 + 100

66. 716 + 100

67. 281 − 100

68. 557 − 100

69. 909 − 100

Work out

1. 185 + 7
2. 639 + 6
3. 243 + 90
4. 867 + 40

5. 312 + 200
6. 478 + 500
7. 80 + 70
8. 300 + 400

9. 43 + 38
10. 69 + 27
11. 78 + 54
12. 86 + 66

13. 636 − 5
14. 756 − 9
15. 224 − 60
16. 475 − 80

17. 597 − 400
18. 941 − 700
19. 160 − 90
20. 140 − 80

21. 100 − 25
22. 100 − 72
23. 112 − 48
24. 153 − 75

Copy and complete.

25. ☐ + 8 = 753
26. ☐ + 50 = 212
27. ☐ + 200 = 679
28. ☐ + 70 = 120

29. ☐ + 27 = 63
30. ☐ + 54 = 147
31. ☐ − 4 = 577
32. ☐ − 70 = 198

33. ☐ − 600 = 400
34. ☐ − 18 = 82
35. ☐ − 67 = 67
36. ☐ − 59 = 48

Work out

37. 567 + 149
38. 385 + 246
39. 439 + 373
40. 776 + 148

41. 450 − 213
42. 938 − 395
43. 562 − 126
44. 849 − 674

Set out correctly and work out.

45. 294 + 267
46. 358 + 175
47. 615 − 367
48. 716 − 289

Work out

49. 5 × 3
50. 7 × 5
51. 8 × 2
52. 6 × 4
53. 9 × 10
54. 4 × 8
55. 20 ÷ 5
56. 10 ÷ 2
57. 80 ÷ 10
58. 36 ÷ 4
59. 18 ÷ 3
60. 56 ÷ 8

61. 80 × 4
62. 70 × 10
63. 90 × 5
64. 60 × 2
65. 50 × 8
66. 40 × 3
67. 180 ÷ 2
68. 600 ÷ 10
69. 280 ÷ 4
70. 240 ÷ 3
71. 720 ÷ 8
72. 250 ÷ 5

Copy and complete.

73. ☐ × 10 = 40
74. ☐ × 3 = 210
75. ☐ × 5 = 30
76. ☐ × 8 = 240

77. ☐ × 4 = 200
78. ☐ × 2 = 20
79. ☐ ÷ 5 = 8
80. ☐ ÷ 4 = 40

81. ☐ ÷ 2 = 70
82. ☐ ÷ 10 = 5
83. ☐ ÷ 8 = 60
84. ☐ ÷ 3 = 9

Work out

85. 48 × 5
86. 37 × 8
87. 49 × 3
88. 27 × 10

Work out

89. 4)92
90. 3)54
91. 5)70
92. 2)74

Set out correctly and work out.

93. 95 × 4
94. 68 × 2
95. 76 × 3
96. 65 × 8
97. 96 ÷ 8
98. 68 ÷ 4
99. 95 ÷ 5
100. 72 ÷ 3

What fraction of each shape is:
a) blue
b) yellow?

1   **5**

2   **6**

3   **7**

4   **8**

Write the fraction shown by each letter.

9

10

11

12

Draw fraction lines like those above to show:

13 quarters

14 sixths

15 eighths

16 twelfths.

Write the larger of each pair of fractions.

17 $\frac{1}{2}$ $\frac{1}{8}$

18 $\frac{1}{4}$ $\frac{1}{3}$

19 $\frac{1}{10}$ $\frac{1}{7}$

20 $\frac{1}{11}$ $\frac{1}{12}$

21 $\frac{2}{5}$ $\frac{3}{5}$

22 $\frac{3}{8}$ $\frac{1}{8}$

23 $\frac{5}{12}$ $\frac{7}{12}$

24 $\frac{5}{9}$ $\frac{4}{9}$

Write the fractions in order, smallest first.

25 $\frac{1}{2}, \frac{1}{9}, \frac{1}{6}$

26 $\frac{7}{10}, \frac{1}{10}, \frac{9}{10}$

27 $\frac{3}{4}, \frac{3}{5}, \frac{3}{10}$

28 $\frac{5}{7}, \frac{6}{7}, \frac{4}{7}$

Copy and complete.

29 $1 = \boxed{}$ quarters

30 $1 = \boxed{}$ eighths

31 $1 = \boxed{}$ thirds

32 $1 = \boxed{}$ tenths

Copy and complete.

33 $1 = \frac{1}{5} + \frac{\boxed{}}{5}$

34 $1 = \frac{8}{12} + \frac{\boxed{}}{12}$

35 $1 = \frac{5}{6} + \frac{\boxed{}}{6}$

36 $1 = \frac{2}{9} + \frac{\boxed{}}{9}$

Copy and complete.

37 $\frac{1}{3} + \frac{1}{3} = \frac{\boxed{}}{3}$

38 $\frac{4}{10} + \frac{5}{10} = \frac{\boxed{}}{10}$

39 $\frac{2}{5} + \frac{\boxed{}}{5} = \frac{3}{5}$

40 $\frac{1}{7} + \frac{\boxed{}}{7} = \frac{5}{7}$

41 $\frac{3}{4} - \frac{2}{4} = \frac{\boxed{}}{4}$

42 $\frac{12}{12} - \frac{5}{12} = \frac{\boxed{}}{12}$

43 $\frac{7}{8} - \frac{\boxed{}}{8} = \frac{4}{8}$

44 $\frac{5}{6} - \frac{\boxed{}}{6} = \frac{2}{6}$

45 Write the fraction shown by each letter:
a) in words
b) in figures.

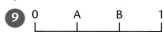

What fraction do you reach?

46 Start at one tenth.
Count on three tenths.

47 Start at seven tenths.
Count back five tenths.

48 Start at three tenths.
Count on six tenths.

49 Start at 1.
Count back nine tenths.

50 Start at two tenths.
Count on four tenths.

Copy and complete.

1 10 cm = ☐ mm

2 5 mm = ☐ cm

3 $\frac{1}{2}$ litre = ☐ ml

4 2 kg = ☐ g

5 1 km 500 m = ☐ m

6 2 m 7 cm = ☐ cm

7 5 litres = ☐ ml

8 1 kg 400 g = ☐ g

Write the measurement shown by each arrow.

9

10

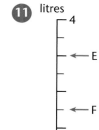

11 litres

Write the answer only.

12 90 cm + 70 cm

13 60 cm − 25 cm

14 83 m + 56 m

15 110 m − 38 m

16 400 ml + 120 ml

17 1000 ml − 550 ml

18 47 kg + 35 kg

19 70 g + 55 g

Measure the edges of each shape to the nearest millimetre. Work out the perimeter.

20

21
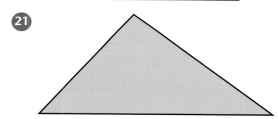

Write the time shown on each clock:

a) in words

b) in figures using am and pm.

22 8:15 morning

23 10:35 night

24 afternoon

25 night

26 How many seconds is 2 minutes?

27 How many minutes is one and a quarter hours?

28 How many days are there in:

a) May

b) June

c) December

d) this year

e) next February

f) 2052?

29 A PE lesson starts at 1:45.
It finishes at 2:25.
How long does it last?

30 A TV programme starts at 4:20.
It lasts 55 minutes.
When does it finish?

Work out the total cost of each pair of items and the change.

31 cake   45p
drink   39p
PAY   £1

32 ice cream   80p
lolly   55p
PAY   £2

33 book   £4·90
pen   £1·20
PAY   £10

34 apples   £1·15
bananas   £1·55
PAY   £5

1 Construct the rectangle. Measure the diagonal AC.

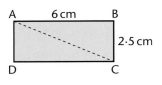

2 Construct the triangle. Measure the side AB to the nearest millimetre.

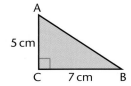

3 How many cubes would be needed to build this cuboid?

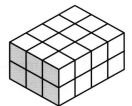

4 How many cubes would be needed to build this cuboid? (Lengths in cubes.)

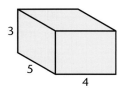

5 How many edges are there in:
a) a triangular based pyramid
b) a cuboid
c) a triangular prism?

6 How many faces are there in:
a) a square based pyramid
b) a cuboid
c) a triangular prism?

7 How many vertices are there in:
a) a cube
b) a triangular prism
c) a triangular based pyramid?

8 Use squared paper. Draw a net for:
a) an open cube
b) a closed cube.

9 How many sides are there in:
a) a pentagon
b) a quadrilateral
c) a hexagon?

Find the new time if the hour hand makes:

10 a 90° turn from 6 o'clock

11 a half turn from 2 o'clock

12 a whole turn from 11 o'clock

13 a 90° turn from 1 o'clock

14 a half turn from 10 o'clock.

15 Decide if each angle A–G is:
a) a right angle
b) an acute angle
c) an obtuse angle.

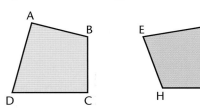

16

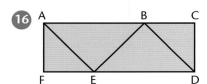

Look at the rectangle. Which line is:
a) parallel to AF
b) perpendicular to BD
c) parallel to AE
d) perpendicular to ED?

17 Look at the rectangle ACDF above. Write down two lines which are:
a) vertical   **b)** horizontal

18 Draw a square with a perimeter of 14 cm.

MENTAL TESTS

TEST 1

1. What is 100 less than 764?

2. Write 3 kg in grams.

3. Kelly spends £1·12. She pays £2. How much change is she given?

4. What is 28 divided by 4?

5. Add 58 and 27.

6. How many minutes make two and a half hours?

7. Write 508 in words.

8. Divide 100 by 10.

9. What is 9 threes?

10. Three fifths of a cake is eaten. What fraction is left?

11. Take 200 from 352.

12. Ice creams cost 70p each. What do two ice creams cost altogether?

13. How many centimetres is 10 m?

14. What is the value of the three in 392?

15. Luke has 48p. He spends 19p. How much does he have left?

16. How many faces does a cube have?

17. What is the sum of 365 and 80?

18. One hundred and eight apples are picked. 34 are rotten. How many can be eaten?

19. Multiply 4 by 8.

20. What number do you reach if you count on four steps of 50 from 0?

21. How many thirds make one?

22. What is the perimeter of a square with sides 6 cm long?

23. How many 5p coins make 60p?

24. What is 60 less than 127?

TEST 2

1. What is 9 times 4?

2. What is the value of the eight in 683?

3. What needs to be added to 46 to make 100?

4. How many 2p coins make 24p?

5. Write 20 mm in centimetres.

6. What is 8 more than 159?

7. Halve 120.

8. How many edges are there in a triangular prism?

9. Add 95 and 17.

10. Raffle tickets cost 25p each. What do 10 tickets cost in pounds and pence?

11. A cake weighs 925 g. 400 g is eaten. How much is left?

12. A lesson starts at 9:40 and finishes at 10:30. How long does it last?

13. What needs to be added to three quarters to make one?

14. Three people share a prize of £150. How much should each receive?

15. What number is 100 more than 702?

16. How many millilitres make 5 litres?

17. Mark has 72p. Ali has 50p. How much do they have altogether?

18. What is the fifth multiple of 8?

19. What number do you reach if you count back four tenths from seven tenths?

20. Write 460 in words.

21. Dawn pays £10 for her shopping. She is given £1·40 change. How much has she spent?

22. How many groups of four can be made from 48 children?

23. Pete's book has 150 pages. He has read seventy. How many pages are left?

24. How many 8s make 88?

How to learn a times table.

BY YOURSELF

1. Read the table over and over.
2. Cover the table and say it out loud or in your mind.
3. Say it more and more quickly.
4. Try to say the table backwards.

WITH A FRIEND

Ask each other questions like:

What is 7 times 3?

Multiply 6 by 4.

How many eights make 40?

Divide 45 by 5.

✕	1	2	3	4	5	6	7	8	9	10	11	12
ONES	1	2	3	4	5	6	7	8	9	10	11	12
TWOS	2	4	6	8	10	12	14	16	18	20	22	24
THREES	3	6	9	12	15	18	21	24	27	30	33	36
FOURS	4	8	12	16	20	24	28	32	36	40	44	48
FIVES	5	10	15	20	25	30	35	40	45	50	55	60
SIXES	6	12	18	24	30	36	42	48	54	60	66	72
SEVENS	7	14	21	28	35	42	49	56	63	70	77	84
EIGHTS	8	16	24	32	40	48	56	64	72	80	88	96
NINES	9	18	27	36	45	54	63	72	81	90	99	108
TENS	10	20	30	40	50	60	70	80	90	100	110	120
ELEVENS	11	22	33	44	55	66	77	88	99	110	121	132
TWELVES	12	24	36	48	60	72	84	96	108	120	132	144